AF256259

Praise for...

If Thoreau Had a Bicycle

"In this lively travelogue, Mark Cramer updates Thoreau's philosophy of walking and nonconformity, as Cramer saunters by bike outside of contemporary Paris. Well past seventy and now post-surgery, Cramer, a cyclist for decades and long-time Paris resident, undertakes a series of rides in "the spirit of undying adventure" (as Thoreau advised the true walker). Where his mentor preached the art of walking, Cramer advocates the art of the ride, logging in the process over one thousand kilometers while embracing the eco-social landscape and diversity of exurban life with an unfailingly warm heart and a critical eye. Thoreau would probably have passed on the chocolate-almond croissants and espresso that sometimes fuel this adventure, but he surely would have relished the result: a witty, provocative, and thoroughly engaging read."

William Rossi, editor of *Walden, Civil Disobedience and Other Writings*, and professor emeritus of American literature and environmental studies, University of Oregon

"Whether you can remember the last time you saw Paris, or not, Mark Cramer's 1,000-kilometer, 39 day-tripper bike ride journey through the beaux villages of France is a meditation on life, the health of our planet, and how two-wheeled travel uses "metabolic energy to replace manufactured energy"—the same way that Henry David Thoreau used a pond 160 years ago to expound on the need for a "tolerable planet." Cramer weaves through "wounded territory," meditating on suburban sprawl, big box stores, "GDP growth oligarchs," and choco-amande pastries. At the end of his ride, the 77-year-old Cramer discovers: "I have been flirting with all the beauty, going too fast…yet a deeper purpose tells me to slow down… Maybe not new destinations but deeper destinations." *If Thoreau Had A Bicycle* is a free-wheeling dive into the richness of momentary experiences that make life worthwhile."

Al Norman, Sprawl-Busters

"As a Dad in a 'Transition Family' with four bikes and zero cars, I devoured Mark Cramer's new book If Thoreau Had a Bicycle. (And it's easy to devour; his crisp, entertaining story races.) Given that political and tech solutions alone will not even begin to heal humanity's appalling imbalance with the rest of Mother Earth, localization and Transition offer a real future. Cramer rightly suggests that anyone can get real in this way—wherever they live and whether on two-wheels or not.

When considering an action, I sometimes ask 'WWTD?' or 'What would Thoreau do?' He'd certainly read this book. Were he alive in 2022, he'd likely have written this future classic."

William Powers, author of the award-winning underground bestseller *Twelve by Twelve: A One Room Cabin, Off the Grid & Beyond the American Dream* and five other books. He lives in Bolivia and helped initiate that country's first Transition Town in 2016.
www.williampowersbooks.com

If Thoreau Had a Bicycle

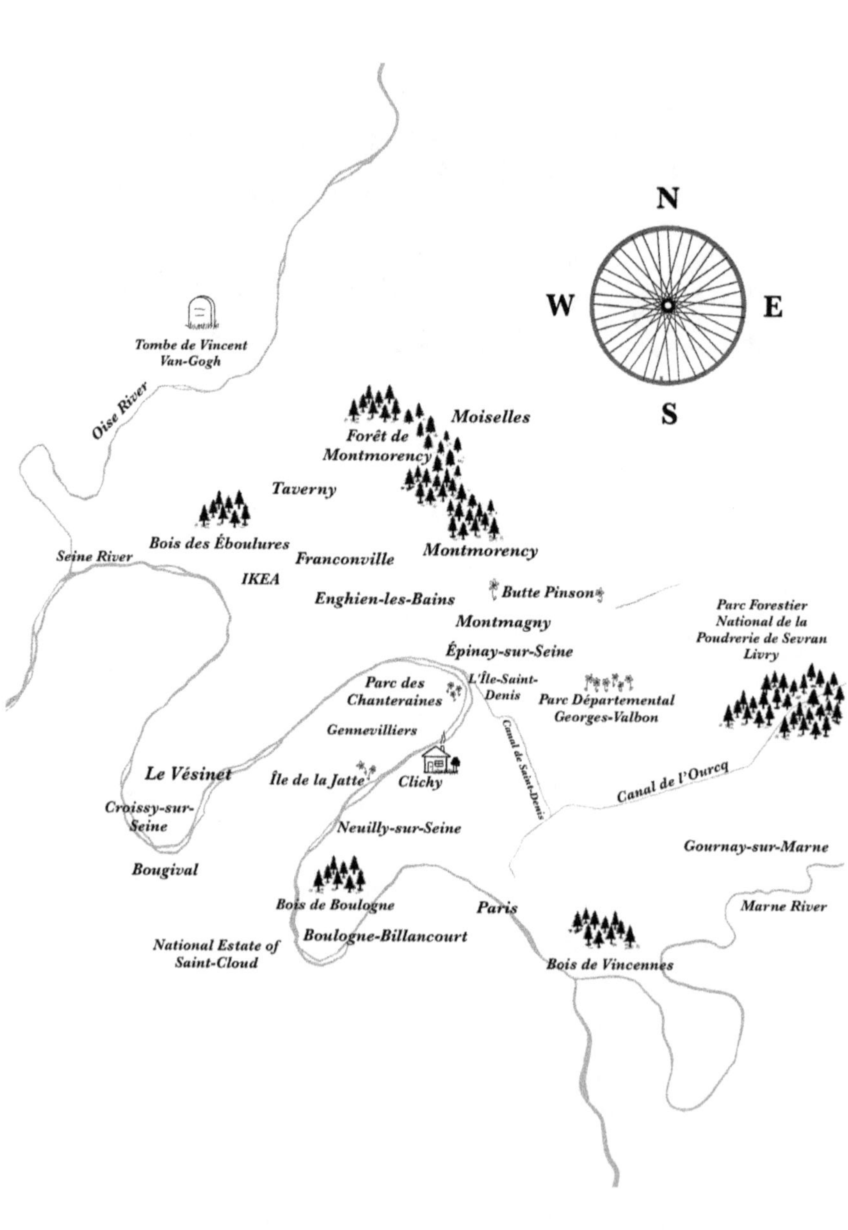

N
W E
S
Tombe de Vincent Van-Gogh
Oise River
Moiselles
Forêt de Montmorency
Taverny
Seine River
Bois des Éboulures
Franconville
IKEA
Montmorency
Enghien-les-Bains
Butte Pinson
Montmagny
Parc Forestier National de la Poudrerie de Sevran
Livry
Épinay-sur-Seine
Parc des Chanteraines
L'Île-Saint-Denis
Parc Départemental Georges-Valbon
Gennevilliers
Canal de Saint-Denis
Le Vésinet
Île de la Jatte
Clichy
Canal de l'Ourcq
Croissy-sur-Seine
Neuilly-sur-Seine
Gournay-sur-Marne
Bougival
Marne River
Bois de Boulogne
Paris
National Estate of Saint-Cloud
Boulogne-Billancourt
Bois de Vincennes

If Thoreau Had a Bicycle

The Art of the Ride

Mark Cramer

Steady State Press
Arlington, VA

If Thoreau Had a Bicycle: The Art of the Ride

ISBN:

Map credit: Rosalie Bull

Photo credits: Canal de l'Ourcq and Saint-Leonard Chapel from Wikimedia Commons. All other photos from Mark Cramer.

Printed in USA

To Alan Kennedy

Contents

Preface

On my 77th birthday, I embarked on a 1,000-kilometer bicycle odyssey, using Henry David Thoreau's essay "Walking" as inspiration, the method for my madness.

I was exploring the implicit connections between Thoreau and steady-state economics, as advocated by Center for the Advancement of the Steady State Economy (CASSE), while identifying with the Transition Movement's respect for ecological resilience and equity. I sensed that Thoreau's writing on simplicity and living close to nature was at least as relevant today as when he penned his essay

The cycling-simplicity-sustainability nexus flowered in me over time. In the 1990s, I was only vaguely aware that limitless growth on a finite planet was not an option, neither on a personal nor a planetary level. For motives entirely self-serving, my wife and I abruptly simplified our existence. By 1995, we no longer owned a car, had radically curtailed our intake of meat and industrial "foods," and had de-stressed our daily lives by shrinking the volume of our housing. To this day, some good folks try to rescue us from this non-consumerist behavior, mistaking our liberating simplicity for sacrifice.

In Paris in 2000, as a millennial resolution, I began daily commuting, rain or shine, by bicycle. Through other utilitarian bicyclers, I discovered the degrowth movement and started reading: *The Limits to Growth* from the Club of Rome, the works of Serge Latouche, André Gorz and Paul Ariès, and later, *"La Décroissance: le Journal de la Joie de Vivre"* as a subscriber. I reread E.F. Schumacher's *Small is Beautiful: Economics as if People Mattered* and the works of Ivan Illich. And I rediscovered and grew to love the writing of Henry David Thoreau, whose core messages I had missed in high school English.

Following the 2008 economic crash, I taught a university class at Sciences-Po in Paris called "Degrowth or Smart Growth?" In preparation, I studied Herman Daly's *Beyond Growth: The Economics of Sustainability*. (Daly would later write the foreword to Brian Czech's *Supply Shock: Economic Growth at the Crossroads and the Steady State Solution* (2013), as the mechanics of degrowth and steady-state economics converged.) By this time, I could see that Thoreau's appealing prescriptions for individual lifestyles could also benefit society and the living earth.

During that period, I was invited to speaking engagements, not as an expert in degrowth theory but as a real-life practitioner. Appropriately, I commuted to these events by bicycle.

Disenchanted by "green growth" and tech solutions, I joined a French association, Attac, that espoused "changing our way of life instead of changing the climate." I reconnected with my American roots through CASSE, GrowthBusters, and Sprawl Busters. Sprawl Busters' fight against big box hegemony made sense since sprawl is the immediate enemy of utilitarian bicycling.

The success of Critical Mass bicycle movements suggests that a critical mass of steady-state way-of-lifers can force open doors for policy experts with alternatives to GDP. They can help spread the truth that the human costs of our current system of uneconomic growth far outweigh any statistical benefits. The words of Robert F. Kennedy still reverberate on YouTube: GDP "measures everything except that which makes life worthwhile."

With Thoreau's walking method as a template, I argue that our regular use of metabolic energy to replace manufactured energy serves our own health and the health of the planet. Of course, even commuters with no intention of using a bike will partake of an environmental dividend when transportation modal share shifts from car use to bicycling and public transit. A simpler mobility compatible with nature can benefit all as part of a steady-state transition.

Thoreau, I believe, would understand, nod in approval, and most probably, climb in the saddle.

Introduction

During my recovery from a double hernia operation, I got the OK from the surgeon to get back on a bike, the permission landing, coincidentally, on my 77th birthday.

He told me to take it slowly and gradually.

I set out on a thousand-kilometer ride.

I asked myself how I'd gotten to this point in my 21st century cycling history. Thoreau had walked into the wild and became a part of its untamed grandeur. By contrast, I was riding through a wounded territory, in search of its remaining sanctuaries and especially the places where nature (both human and ecoregional) was fighting back.

It was a race of endurance: my own vulnerable human microbiome allied with the increasingly depleted Euro-Atlantic mixed-forest freshwater ecoregion. Nature and I were taking on the GDP growth oligarchs who were trampling us in the name of "the economy."

The most perverse among them even planned to migrate to new worlds beyond our atmosphere, evacuating an Earth that they were destroying knowingly.

I considered two possible motives for my urge to get back on a bike. Was I driven by a desire to be in true harmony with nature? Or was I acting under the influence of the consumerist desire for accumulation?

If gluttony is eating overindulged, what is excessive cycling called? I have a long cycling history, but I can't seem to get enough. I have cycled the Loire castle region and along the canals in Bruges, Belgium, with my wife Martha. Alone or with cycling partners, I've done the Compiegne forests, the Normandie hills and beaches, Barcelona's beaches and hills,

Cascais in Portugal on a one-speed bike, Santa Clarita's dry river trails in California, Cárdenas in Cuba, the bicycle commuting of the Paris region (for 15 years), and literally "above all," the canyons around La Paz, Bolivia at 12,000 feet, where Martha has family.

How could I want more? The surgeon had put me on a mild cycling diet. I probed the potential pathology of my mindset.

Eating : Gluttony = Bicycling : _________?

Binge Pedaling? Road Craving? Pavement Rage? Age Denialism? Nihilism on the Move?

My first thousand K'er coincided with the 2010 Tour de France. I reached the 1,000 km charity commitment, along with my cycling partner, Alan Kennedy, and on our 21st day, arriving at the Arc de Triomphe to meet the Tour finishers, even though the Tour finishers had no interest in meeting us. Compared to us, the Tour competitors had cycled half the time but eaten up four times the distance. But in contrast to Tour de France riders, we got to stop and see things along the way.

My second 1,000 km ride was in autumn 2019, this time to promote human-fueled travel as a replacement for manufactured energy and to document rural "*desertification*" in parts of France. This mainly-solo ride was written up by the French environmental organization, Attac92; I appreciated having Attac activists Claire and Elie join me on a 70 km segment.

For one 40 km ride, I'd held off on my morning coffee so I could sip it at a classic village café. However, in each beautiful town along the way, shutters were down, streets barren. The French *beaux villages* had been reduced to stunning solitude. I gawked at the grainy façades with colorful shutters. I wondered how this historic beauty was on the verge of dying. The melancholy was as thick as the profuse foliage lining the Epte river.

When I reached the town of my overnight *auberge* in Normandy, still longing for a coffee, the village priest invited me for a beer.

The priest explained why I'd found nothing open. "Many towns have been gutted commercially because of online competition," he said, "even if the process started with the big box stores" (*grands surfaces*). The online commerce share of GDP was growing frenetically, yet it left entire regions in despair by displacing labor-intensive local businesses.

A week later, on a hilly rural road outside of Compiègne, I came upon a mail carrier who had stopped her yellow La Poste truck to feed two donkeys. I braked at the junction of two richly silent rural roads. Following the *"Bonjour madame,"* I quoted the priest, asking whether the online phenomenon had an impact on her job.

"Soon we will all be employees of Amazon." She smiled while caressing the donkeys.

That 2019 off-the-grid voyage supported Attac's actions against planned obsolescence with my 20-year-old bike as a symbol of "better fix than discard". That exhilarating journey served to prolong my "state of denial" regarding the inevitable obsolescence of the human body.

During an October-November 2021 family visit, I cycled in the environs of the canyon city of La Paz, Bolivia, consisting entirely of climbs and descents, at 12,000 feet above sea level. I began to believe that I had staved off obsolescence, that I could tinker with my body mechanics to increase my healthy life expectancy.

However, the hernia operation in March of 2022 forced me to reckon with the fact that, like a cotton gin, a cell phone, a phonograph, a telegraph, an 8-track or a Cadillac, my biological machine would eventually wear down and die off. I compared my surgeon to one of those Cuban mechanics who manage to keep 1950s Fords and Chevys on the streets. My surgeon had put me back on the road.

Rules of the Road

For my new, post-surgery 1,000 km ride, I set down some simple rules based on my view of bicycling as an artistic endeavor, in accord with Thoreau's approach to "the art of walking" (260). (All subsequent Thoreau quotes are from *Walden, Civil Disobedience, and Other Writings*, edited by William Rossi (Third Edition, 2008) unless otherwise noted.)

I would be departing each day from our apartment (a mere campground in the cosmic scheme of things), but in daily segments, would recreate the magic of a cross-continental bike trip.

Rule One: Each outing must have a new destination, a place worthy of a stopover on a road trip, to help create the illusion of a long trip.

No grinding out mileage in velodromic circularity. The ride must include the wonders of geographic sensoriality.

Beginning in Clichy, France, just north of Paris, I had six sets of "escape routes," as I came to think about these rides. For me they symbolized escape from the accepted norm of perpetual growth. Each set, heading in a different direction, branched out into a multitude of excursions:

(1) North: The Gennevilliers bridge over the Seine took me in the direction of the expansive Montmorency Forest and the Oise River.

(2) Northwest: The Clichy bridge, with new bike lanes thanks to COVID measures, took me to *La Seine à Vélo*, a car-free river ride that could meander as far as the beaches of Normandy.

(3) West: Clichy's own "left bank" of the Seine River took me past the American Hospital of Paris (in case I broke down), through the expansive Boulogne Forest, and beyond.

(4) South into Paris: Here I use the widened bike lane implanted to decongest the Metro.

(5) East: Using the Paris outer boulevard bike lane, this route would lead me to the Canal de l'Ourcq, a waterway towpath that extends into eastern France.

(6) "No-go zones": I would venture into terra incognita in search of a sixth escape route.

Rule One logistics: I wanted to prove that bicycling makes for a remarkably accessible form of touring that can serve people more efficiently than fueled transport.

The mission was to "create" a road trip, showing readers how they can do the *same from their own front door*. By localizing the joys of travel, we are cutting down on manufactured energy while improving quality of life.

I questioned whether it would be possible to find 40 different destinations within bicycling distance when departing from the same place. I reasoned that if Thoreau could achieve this on foot, it should be easier on a bike. Consider the words of Henry David Thoreau: "My vicinity affords many good walks; and though for so many years I have walked almost every day, and sometimes for several days together, I have not yet exhausted them." (264)

Given the effects of suburban sprawl after Thoreau's lifetime, only an artistic approach could carve out 40 destinations.

Rule Two: Find the artistic balance between Don't force it and Challenge the body. Prove that incremental increases in distance, speed and exertion can rejuvenate my un-endowed human body. Define my limits and coexist with them, but do not succumb to them.

Incrementalism meant beginning my initial outings in lower gears of my simple 7-speed bike, gradually increasing average daily distance, elevation gains, and frequency of bouts of intense exertion. As the symptoms of fatigue decreased, I would be transitioning to pre-surgery gear levels.

I was heeding the words of the novelist and marathon runner Haruki Murakami: "Muscles are like work animals that are quick on the uptake. If you carefully increase the load step by step, they learn to take it… As long as you take your time and do it in stages, they'll very patiently and obediently grow stronger." I intended to add my personal anecdotal evidence that people who are not biologically intended to be ultra-athletes can get into great shape through incremental challenges.

I outlined three travel modes:

(1) *Steady-state*: Pedaling with ease, what exercise physiologist Dr. Stephen Seiler aptly calls "the green zone." Seiler assures us that we gain in endurance even when riding in the green zone and that most exercise should be in the green zone; otherwise we will be in overreach.

(2) *Flexible-state*: Equivalent to intensity intervals in high-intensity interval training (HIIT), except that I would let geography and necessity determine when those high-intensity moments would occur.

(3) *Unsustainable growth*: Cycling beyond my capacity, either out of necessity, like pedaling full throttle to arrive at a shelter before an incoming thunderstorm, or for the joy of a challenge, like battling some tough hills for the peak experience of making

it to the top. Such overreach would degrade my physical condition if it became habitual, like infinite growth on a finite planet, but could offer an enriching challenge when limited to peak experiences.

Rule Three ("The Third Chair"): Depend on the locals, the living social network. By traveling off the grid, without a phone, I would forego the selfie independence that shutters one off from other members of the species. I would thrive on my sense of direction, getting help from locals if I got lost.

I am loosely developing this theme, triggered by a quote from Thoreau's *Walden*: "I had three chairs in my house; one for solitude, two for friendship, three for society." (97) The third chair was for the unexpected social connection, less defined than friendship.

In 2021, the mobile phone industry contributed 4.5 trillion U.S. dollars to global GDP, a whopping 5% of total global GDP, according to Statista, "Global mobile industry contribution to GDP worldwide from 2014 to 2025."

The mining of smartphone components is profoundly disturbing: it contaminates the atmosphere, severely damages ecosystems, and relies on hyper-exploitation of miners. It leaves toxic byproducts oozing into the soil and water.

Today phone-free has become a greater challenge than car-free. If confronting the cell-phone culture, would Thoreau have declared, "But lo! men have become the tools of their tools" (29)?

Please note that this phone-free third chair approach is experimental. I cannot preach to my fellow sentient beings that they ditch their cell-phone because if they have an accident and do not have a phone to call for help, it will be my fault.

What would Thoreau have done? "Most of the luxuries," he wrote, "and many of the so-called comforts in life, are not only not indispensable, but positive hindrances to the elevation of mankind" (13).

Statistically, people are not proven to be happier when hooked into and hacked by digital conveniences. Mathematically, people must work longer hours to pay for redefining one-time luxuries as indispensable conveniences. Convenience has a price.

The cell phone has become an integral part of the human body. In the year 2000, half the passengers on Paris metro trains were reading books. Today, most passengers are using their smart phones. Where is this taking us as a species?

Traveling off the grid, I'll use paper contour maps, which enhance my sense of place. GPS is a great tool, but it creates dependency. Visitors arrive at our apartment by way of Google maps without a minimal notion of how they got there or even whether they've gone north or south. I understand why bicycle advocate Ryan Van Duzer uses electronic maps when he rides trails in the middle of nowhere. If I were in Baja California, I would too. But on my daily trips, I want to spread out a map on the dining room table and revel in the entire context of the ride.

For photos, I'll depend on the generosity of the locals. This will involve chance interactions. How many people will be willing to stop, take pictures of someone resembling *The Stranger* of Camus, and then send those images to the stranger's email?

The locals, I hope, will also help me find the things I need and point the way if I get lost. Instead of locating shops, services, or museums on the internet, why not consult the living social network around me: the third chair?

The Art of the Ride

Bike riding as an art relates to music more than any other art form. It cannot stand still on a canvas nor be lifted on a pedestal in a public square. It gets close to dance when mountain bikers do it, but bicycling moves through time, to symphonic destinations, with rhythmic variations.

In bike riding, the simple melody, moving forward while changing rhythms, is accompanied by the harmonies of the habitat. The bicycle tourist merges with both harmonic and dissonant landscapes.

Maintaining the illusion (or creating a new reality) of a legitimate road trip was facilitated by having a variety of escape routes to choose from.

My five distinct departure routes from Clichy branched into dozens of others. By alternating these routes, each ride would truly have the feel of the new day of a road trip.

My magical reality voyage was threatened, however, when having to return to my base camp. Even when varying the return routes, I feared a letdown when ending up at home. Thoreau expressed some anguish about returning to "the old hearth-side." But he conjured up a solution: "We should go forth on the shortest walk, perchance, in the spirit of undying adventure, never to return; prepared to send back our embalmed hearts only, as a relic to our desolate kingdoms" (261).

Thoreau created his illusion of being "free from all worldly engagements" by sauntering through woods and fields for at least four hours per day. Once recovered, I would adopt his four-hour strategy.

I would develop tricks to minimize the hearth-side letdown. For example, long-distance bikepackers must find their food, water, and supplies on the road before staking out a campsite. I resolved to hunt and gather for my daily necessities *during* my trips rather than waiting to do so from home.

In the 1800s, the first great American environmentalist, Henry David Thoreau, did not have a bike. If he were alive today, he'd be riding one, for utilitarian, artistic, philosophical, and ecological reasons, as we shall see in the chronicles that follow. We only need to repeat his mantra to understand that as a proponent of both human energy and a joyously frugal economy, Thoreau would be an advocate for a steady state economy that refuses to exceed ecological limits. Let's repeat the mantra of this bicycle voyage:

> If a man walks in the woods for love of them half of each day, he is in danger of being regarded as a loafer; but if he spends his whole day as a speculator, shearing off those woods and making earth bald before her time, he is esteemed an industrious and enterprising citizen. (Life Without Principle, 1863)

First Movement: Adagio

Days 1 through 7

Warm-up

The first movement must advance slowly. The mysterious conversion of simple bacteria into complex mitochondria took uncountable ages. I need to respect these mitochondria at work in my body, as a source of power that was crafted from immense patience. I cannot force them in the early going.

If I am to encourage my fellow citizens of all ages and abilities to become active like Thoreau, they need to know that the adventure can have an unsensational but sweet beginning. The getting-started phase of an extended physical challenge is when people are more likely to drop out. The best way to prevent discouragement is to have fun.

Day 1

Against Traffic
on a One-Way Street

For my first day back on the bike following surgery, I decide to take a short spin just to make sure that I can go out and come back in one piece with no need for a painkiller. My plan is to cycle on a new branch of my western route with only four blocks on surface streets before the route eases into protected bike lanes along the Seine.

The first block, the get-away, involves riding against the traffic on a one-way street. Legally! In our region, one-way streets with 30 km/hr speed limits allow for bike riders to "contra-flow" against the traffic. Painted lanes or mid-street bicycle decals signal that this is legal. It's also proven to be safe.

We can see the cars coming and, if necessary, we can move over. Better than hearing the unseen terror of noisy engines approaching from behind. Experiments with the contra-flow streets began back in 2010 in Paris with car drivers having had more than a decade to handle the culture shock. My perception is that with these contra-flow streets, car drivers have gained empathy for bicycle riders. And it works the other way around as well.

On the contra-flow streets, when a car heads toward me, I don't expect a honk or an angry shout. Often, I get an understanding nod.

This significant infrastructure enhancement did not come from the void. The trigger dates back to 1992, when a loosely-constituted gathering called Critical Mass in San Francisco initiated monthly political-protest rides, occupying streets to demand both their fair share of street space and clean air. These rides were acts of nonviolent civil disobedience, tracing back to a tradition created by Thoreau.

Within a decade, Critical Mass and spin-off organizations with a similar philosophy had spread to 300 different cities around the world. I was first influenced by a Parisian Critical Mass replica called *Vélorution* back in 2001.

Though he predated common bicycle travel, an essential bicycle activist argument can be traced directly to Henry David Thoreau. This is the concept of *effective speed*, originating in Thoreau's *Walden* (1854).

A friend of Thoreau suggests they take the train, to see the country and visit the town of Fitchburg. Thoreau challenges his friend, insisting it would be faster to walk:

> I have learned that the swiftest traveler is he that goes afoot. The distance is thirty miles; the fare ninety cents. That is a day's wages … I start now on foot and get there before night … You will in the meantime have earned your fare [by working], and arrive there some time tomorrow, or possibly this evening if you are lucky enough to get a job in season. (39)

The employment hours needed by Thoreau's friend to pay the fare are factored into the travel time.

In advocating for the efficiency of bicycle travel, Ivan Illich's *Energy and Equity* (1974) draws directly from Thoreau to show that the real time for car travel must include the time spent working in order to pay for the car and its expenses:

> The typical American male devotes more than 1,600 hours a year to his car. He sits in it while it goes and while it stands idling. He parks it and searches for it. He earns the money to put down on it and to meet the monthly instalments. He works to pay for petrol, tolls, insurance, taxes and tickets…The average American

male puts in 1,600 hours to get 7,500 miles, less than five miles per hour. (30-31)

Illich highlights that this is slower than the speed of a bicycle.

In *Slow Cities: Conquering our Speed Addiction for Health and Sustainability* (2020), Paul Tranter, with co-author Rodney Tolley, calculates the Thoreau and Illich idea of net speed, showing that the effective car travel speed in cities like London and New York is slower than an average bicycle speed.

Thoreau's *Walden* and *Civil Disobedience* are mostly perceived as separate subjects, the first environmental and the second as protest against slavery and foreign wars. However, the ecological social movements of bicycle activists blend both Thoreau's activism and his nature writing.

It is this activism that obligated municipal leaders in the Paris region to re-do street infrastructure, including the addition of contra-flow streets, with clean air as the goal. As mode share of bike commuting increased, car commuting would decrease, and the result would be less pollution.

Environmental concerns thus interact with civil disobedience to get this job done. Given that Thoreau promoted effective speed, it is certain that he would have ridden a bike if bicycles had been commonplace in his time.

With my 1,000 km project, I intend to prove that we can get to whatever Fitchburgs in our region, more efficiently, and with greater pleasure, on a bike.

I have not gone far today, but I've gained energy from the symbolism of the contra-flow streets and the fully protected bike lane along the river. I'm feeling fine, but I rode with one gear lower than normal. Still, it's good to know that when all externalities are considered, my slow cycling is still faster than driving a car, and those collateral car costs do not even calculate the health care costs originating from a car-centric sedentary lifestyle.

Day 1: 8 km.

Day 2

The Anti-Quarantine

The word "quarantine" comes from the French word *quarante*, or 40. The original definition was 40 days of isolation, usually indoors. I re-label my trip "the anti-quarantine." My travel is outdoors for 40 days, and it reestablishes social links rather than curtailing them.

For some bike riders, the social links to cycling include the etiquette and functionality of specialty garments. I use no special cycling apparel. Thoreau backs me up: "A man who has at length found something to do will not need a new suit to do it in. For him the old will do … for an indeterminate period." (19)

A friend had sent me a trendy cycling jersey, the type that bike racers use. But I am competing against no one except my own biological limitations. This is the green jersey worn by the Tour de France sprint leader. It seems foolish to be wearing this jersey when an elderly woman suffering from Parkinson's has "outsprinted" me at the corner of Wagram and Villiers.

The forecast is high 60s to low 70s for the entire week, so I reason that I can afford one more prep day and still enjoy the gentle weather when the real challenges begin.

This is my "day without." I cycle to and from Parc des Chanteraines without climbing the elongated wooded hill, without circling around to the birdwatching station, without going to the turtle pond at the end of the park, without cycling up a steep lookout path to delight in a cluster of wild apple trees, which will not be producing their fruit for another five months.

This is equivalent to dining out with no aperitif, no spices added, and no dessert. It is straight and mainly flat through the center of the park.

I miss the ascent to the crab apples, which seem to have re-wilded themselves following centuries of grafting into cultured orchard apples, as the cultivated Thoreau has returned to the wild. Later this afternoon, I plan to reread Thoreau's *Wild Apples*: "…our wild apple is wild only like myself, perchance, who belong not to the aboriginal race here, but have strayed into the woods from the cultivated stock" (295).

On both departure and return, I take the greenway, hardly seeing a motor vehicle except for the Gennevilliers bridge crossing, where my experience with vehicular cycling helps me get onto the bridge by hand signaling to car drivers who seek the same space.

On a similar bridge approach in Miami, Los Angeles, or La Paz, Bolivia, I would not have the same trust in those members of my species who feel fossil-fueled power in their veins. I would need to engage in on-the-spot driver education to secure the space that I legally have a right to under the rules of vehicular cycling.

On this ride, the bridge crossing becomes the sole challenge. I've overcome temptations to treat myself to spirited hill climbs and bursts of speed. I need this "breezing workout", as they say in horse racing. A trainer does not want to overextend his horse in preparation for a real challenge.

I practice what I've preached: an incremental approach in the steady-state mode. But I will soon have to cycle an average of 30 km per day to make up for the short distances of this "adagio" period.

The anti-quarantine process has just begun. I've gotten home too soon, and without the usual socializing at the bird-watching post or snack stand. I resolve to return to Chanteraines at a later stage for a more roundabout and deeper *parcours*.

Day 2: 12 km. Trip to date: 20 km.

Day 3

Mint-and-Chip Ice Cream

From my front door, it's exactly 10 km to a point along the Seine à Vélo that will later serve as a gateway to adventure, but for now, must become a truncated destination.

There will be great temptations at the 10 km point, under the Pont de Bezons, to roll farther along the car-free route to pretty villages down river. But my rigorous incrementalist pledge is non-negotiable.

With my Rule One, each destination requires a fulfilled temptation. In my largely but not exclusively plant-based whole-food diet, I'd be scorned by the vegans. I allow myself an unprescribed non-wholesome pleasure so long as I have worked to get it. Dear vegan friends, surely a scoop of ice cream is not unhealthy if earned with a 20 km bike ride.

Following my escape over the Clichy bridge bike lane and 7 km of mostly protected bike paths through Gennevilliers (see Day 6: Behind the Iron Curtain), I've reached the next meander of the Seine and the convivial Seine à Vélo greenway. I feel my first waves of bicycle liberation. Amongst senior strollers, zigzagging scooters, intense joggers, nature bloggers, and Herculean weightlifters, I am shape-shifting amidst a big bang of humanity. Outpacing a slow barge on my right, I sense the flow of the river in my easy breathing as I morph into something new. True, I'm not going fast, but I roll forward with much more fluidity than on the first two days.

At the snack stand, I have to make one of those on-the-road decisions. Instead of "to buy or rent" or "to be or not to be," it is "pistachio or mint-and-chip?" This is what I love about bike touring: the banal decisions, confined to the "right now."

I choose a scoop of the mint-and-chip. I remember the Bill Moyers documentary on Buddhism that taught me to eat slowly. I allow for no distractions as I savor each creamy bite of the mint-and-chip. I ignore the river, ignore the tall trees bending in the breeze, ignore the shouting kids in the distance, ignore that I am a particle within a big bang.

It is only this slow scoop of ice cream.

Day 3: 20 km. Trip to date: 40 km.

Day 4

Finding Hemingway

In the 1920s, Ernest Hemingway played the horse races at Auteuil in the Boulogne Forest. In his 1964 memoir, *A Moveable Feast,* Hemingway writes about his problematic years as a writer in Paris of the 1920s. We get to meet people he loved and hated and places where he hung out, many of which are still here in Paris today.

The place that gets left out of most Hemingway-in-Paris reviews is Auteuil. I decide to bicycle out to Auteuil to relive some of Hemingway's intense moments. After all, he was a serious horseplayer and sometimes depended on a winning horse for his next meal.

Auteuil's old grandstand, where Hemingway hung out, has survived the tests of real estate speculation, having been declared an historic monument. In fact, the newer grandstand was built to harmonize with the old one.

In Hemingway's life of calculated risk, racing fit within his philosophy. It was with great sorrow that he gave it up, as recounted in *A Moveable Feast.*

Modern pari-mutuel racing was first introduced to the world on Auteuil's opening day in 1873. In those days with little in the way of published past performances, the player had to be at the track to watch all the races and take notes on each horse. Hemingway realized that this constituted a full-time job and rather than do it in a shabby way, he ultimately gave it up, calling racing "my demanding friend." One of the ways to replace his demanding friend was bicycling, so it made symbolic sense for me to visit his grandstand by bicycle. He wrote:

> It is by riding a bike that you learn the contours of a country best, since you have to sweat up the hills and coast down them. Thus you remember them as they actually are, while in a motor car, only a high hill impresses you, and you'll have no such accurate remembrance of country you have driven through as you gain by riding a bike. (William White, "By-line Ernest Hemingway," 1967, 364)

On this splendid spring afternoon, I've adopted the Hemingway method: watching a few races and taking notes on each horse. It has been fun, but very demanding indeed.

On my return home, Hemingway helps me appreciate the contours, but he also has given me a winning tip: I need to do more hills.

Day 4: 20 km. Trip to date: 60 km.

Day 5

The Theory of Bicycle Relativity

Utilitarian cycling blends with bicycle touring. It can be as simple as a 20 km ride to get my favorite ice cream or, as today, a foray into Paris to change US dollars to euros. Today will be limited to 12 km round trip but will include the first of what I hope will be many climbs. In riding to the place with the best dollar-euro exchange rates, the last four blocks will consist of a relatively challenging hill up to Champs-Elysées.

On the way, I discover with horror that the narrower of protected bike lanes are no longer 100% safe. Two changes could not have been anticipated by city planners.

In the wake of the COVID peak, bike delivery services have mushroomed throughout the region. For these guys on bikes, every ride has a deadline. They muscle by me in tight quarters. I can no longer be rolling along, singing a song.

Motorized scooters fly by silently like predator pterodactyls. They mean no harm, but their ubiquitous presence has caused me to press the stress button, to remain rigidly in an imaginary lane within the lane.

At certain moments, I long for the days of vehicular cycling.

A third change in the fluid mechanics of bicycle physics now shakes me. A woman, perhaps a few years younger than I, cycles up from behind and draws beside me on my inside. We exchange glances of senior solidarity, then she glides by me effortlessly.

I'm suddenly shaken. How am I going to climb that looming hill if I have become a slowpoke in relation to a bicycler of my own generation? Evidently, she senses my shock and slows down until I roll up to her.

"*Ne vous inquietez-pas.*" She smiles. ("Don't be upset") "*Je suis assistée,*" she explains, pointing to the battery on her e-bike.

I engrave her words, wishing I could have a reasonable response at this moment, but I am a slow thinker. "It will come to me," I think.

We chat side-by-side for the next two blocks, and then she's off like the Concorde. But the damage is done. Passed by carnivorous deliverymen, passed by shooting scooters, passed by skiing e-bikes, I begin to wonder if I have it in me to climb that hill.

In fact, I begin rationalizing that in this first week of post-surgery cycling, I might need to walk the bike partway up that hill.

I am subjected to the miracle of the physics of bicycle relativity. In the final four blocks from Place des Ternes to Place Charles de Gaulle, I meet up with a heavy traffic jam. Within a wide protected bike lane, I cycle up that hill effortlessly. Yes, at a slow pace that would satisfy my surgeon, yet faster than the bogged down cars and trucks to my left!

Thank you, cars and trucks, for reminding me of the Theory of Bicycle Relativity.

And in a happy convergence of relativities, I discover that my dollars have gained value in relation to the euro. I collect my euros, saying "*muchisimas gracias*" to the Mexican woman behind the bulletproof window.

The downhill cruise home is revitalizing. The mysterious force of gravity takes and then gives back. I educate my cosmologist friend, who expresses amazement at how gravity holds together a vast universe. I help him get his priorities straight. More important is that gravity gets us home on a bike with ease and empowerment.

I wish I could find the lady on the electric bike to tell her what I should have said during our encounter: "*Je suis aussi assisté*" (I too am assisted), by a mysterious force that needs no rare earth minerals for its manufacture.

I have two more days of my medically imposed 7-day Adagio before I extend the distance of my daily outings to at least 30 km per day.

Day 5: 12 km. Trip to date: 72 km.

Day 6

Behind the Iron Curtain

Two of my escape routes pass through the city of Gennevilliers: the first one over the Gennevilliers Bridge, the east side of the city, and the second over the Clichy Bridge, which continues over a bicycle path under a comforting tree canopy lined by high rise public housing, on the west side of Gennevilliers.

In my northward escape, either of the two bridges can connect with a third mid-city passage: the Coulée Vert (greenway): a slice of parkland converted into a car-free "boulevard" with a dirt path on either side protected by a profuse tree canopy.

On this outing, my goal is to catch a glimpse of the jackrabbits during their morning run at the Parc de l'Ile Saint-Denis.

Gennevilliers is a working-class city. The population includes a high percentage of immigrants from both Sub-Saharan Africa and the Arabic-speaking countries of the North African Maghreb.

The city offers enough independent services and cultural activities to remain independent from Paris: a major theatre, an independent cinema with foreign films from around the world, and a renovated downtown that restores the typical French townscape, not as a touristy *olde towne,* but a center of local commerce and public services.

It would likely surprise many American readers that this municipality has functioned under communist administrations since the end of World War II.

Gennevilliers is part of the "red suburbs" (*banlieues rouges*): communist municipalities that have surrounded Paris since the end of World War II. Today, only four municipalities still have communist mayors in my Hauts-de-Seine department: Bagneux, Malakoff, Nanterre and Gennevilliers.

It was natural for the communists to exert their influence in the red suburbs since these were working-class communities. Communists had been notably active in the grassroots French resistance against the Nazis.

Today, French communist municipalities are essentially social democrat like any other moderate left government. Communist municipalities have subsidized art cinemas at affordable prices. These independent movie houses continue to flourish after communist municipal governments are replaced by Greens or Socialists.

Clint Eastwood once came to Gennevilliers, precisely along my bike path, to film a scene for his 2018 film, *The 5:17 to Paris*, about the thwarted terrorist attack aboard the Thalys train from Belgium to Paris. He chose to film in the Les Agnettes neighborhood of Gennevilliers because it reminded him of East Berlin. Once he'd installed his crew, according to the daily *Le Parisien*, (25 Aug 2017), Eastwood propped up the immediate neighborhood to look like East Berlin and filmed some bicycling scenes.

"He's not here to promote our youth," said local resident Benjamin. "I hope he will not stigmatize us as a no-go zone."

Since two of my five main exit *parcours* passed through Gennevilliers, I will have ample opportunities to get a feel for the city.

The Coulée Vert is a pleasure for "slow bicycling" advocates. The municipality applies wild gardening and low maintenance principles that Thoreau would likely have approved. Thoreau's essay *Walking* doubles as a treatise in favor of what is wild. He writes of this "vast, savage, howling mother of ours, Nature," and he laments:

> We are so early weaned from her breast to society, to that culture, which is exclusively the interaction of man on man, a sort

of breeding in and in, which produces at most a sort of English nobility, a civilization destined to have a speedy limit. (281)

To the immediate north of Gennevilliers is the small island city of L'Ile Saint-Denis (see Day Fifteen). This city also had communist mayors until 2020, when a mayor with no party affiliation was elected. The Parc de L'Ile Saint-Denis, with the Seine on both sides, has a few wild sections. I was able to catch a glimpse of the jackrabbits scampering across the path, but even as an oasis in an industrial zone, it is a bit too tidy for what Thoreau would have wanted.

Thoreau on a bike, however, would have appreciated the packed dirt paths, the colony of magpies, the unkempt and shady banks of the Seine, and a few mildly steep hills that allowed for a natural change in pedaling rhythm.

For my return, I skip the greenway, cycling back through Clint Eastwood's East Berlin. I formulate a message for the film director. Soviet housing has French roots. The USSR hosted the French-Swiss architect Le Corbusier three times, and Le Corbusier's ideas were extremely popular among Soviet modernist architects.

Le Corbusier once planned to raze an entire neighborhood in, what is today, the thriving Le Marais district of Paris. The local residents successfully rallied against his high-rise *Plan Voisin*. Le Marais is now one of the great neighborhoods of the world with vibrant street life and well-preserved historic buildings.

From my protected bike lane, I look around at the authoritarian prisonlike projects--what Le Corbusier proudly called "living machines." Here and there I see alternative spaces popping up: art centers, convivial cafés, and people creating ad hoc streets out of what were once inhospitable open spaces.

This is human nature sprouting up, insisting on breaking through the cement.

Day 6: 18 km. Trip to date: 90 km.

Day 7

Longchamp

Bicycle-road-racers work out every day around the perimeter of the Longchamp racecourse in bright jerseys pockmarked with advertisements. They never stop to watch a horse race. A bird's eye view would show parallel flows of bright colors within a green forest: jockey silks on the inside circumference, bike racing jerseys on the outside.

I wonder whether I belong more to the bicycle culture on the outer perimeter or the racing culture within. Perhaps I am the missing link between the two subcultures.

The only American horse race trainer in France, Gina Rarick, has a horse running at Longchamp. The racecourse is a 10 km ride via the Boulogne Forest. I've followed her career and written about her courageous adventure that pitted her against the highest odds. As a journalist, Gina had written a *NY Times* sports blog about our 1,000 km bike trip of 2010. When she decided to train horses, she set aside her career as a journalist.

During long periods, Madame Rarick's horses were profitable to bet on with an average return on investment in the black. Lately, she's been in a discouraging slump, and I've decided to show up as a fan to encourage her filly, Ameera. Judging from her *Paris-Turf* past performances, Ameera does not have much of a chance, but during the past calendar year, Rarick had pulled off two upsets with 70-to-1 horses.

I am particularly inspired by Gina's resilience. She wakes up at sunrise to gallop her horses or takes them out to a paddock where they can jump and roam. She makes grinding trips to dozens of racetracks, often with horses that have little chance to win, even if they are in great shape.

The last time I'd been to Longchamp, I'd registered a complaint about the absence of bike parking facilities. When I arrive two races before Ameera is to run, I'm pleased to see that bike parking rails have been installed. To my satisfying surprise, I count 45 bikes parked outside the entrance. I am not alone.

Ironically, all the bike bars are occupied, so I have to chain my bike to a fence.

I make one wager prior to Ameera's race. In a bet called the Multi, I need the top four finishers in any order in a 15-horse field. My horses finish 1st, 2nd, 3rd and 5th, great handicapping with zero return for the effort.

I stroll back to the stable area to say hello to Gina. She flashes a broad smile, optimistic that Ameera will run well. In her underfunded stable, positivity is the best tool for long-term survival. I tell her to say hello to her husband Tim, a fellow bicycle rider.

Gina is doubtful about defeating the race favorite, but she hopes to finish in the top three. I've seen at least seven other horses that have a better chance than Ameera, but I say nothing to discourage her. After all, she's a hands-on trainer, and I do not want to say anything that might diminish her magic touch.

In the walking circle prior to the race, Ameera is acting up, using some of the energy she needs to conserve for the race. As a symbolic gesture I make a small *placé* wager on Ameera (*placé* yields a payoff if the horse finishes in the top three).

Ameera breaks well from the gate and presses the early speed horse from the outside, but visually, the pace looks too fast for her to handle. She weakens before the stretch, and the rider decides not to force the filly when the cause is lost.

Pedaling on my way home, I have a lot to think about. I'm in the final outing of my Adagio period, and I feel ready to seek climbing challenges while boosting the average number of daily kilometers.

Like Gina, I am in it for the long run, but she has bills to pay while I bicycle for free. Her fortunes are tied to a fiercely competitive business and need financial backers. I have total control over my own stamina. Unlike Ameera, I am able to pedal at my own comfortable pace.

If I get passed by *mamils* (middle-aged men in lycra), it makes no difference to me.

I'd wanted to buy a racehorse through Gina. But Martha vetoed the project.

"You have a better chance betting on the horses than owning them," she contended with her usual objectivity.

In Ameera's subsequent race, she finished second, less than a length from winning it all, earning purse money that would help pay the bills.

Day 7: 20 km. Trip to date: 110 km.

Second Movement:
Waterways

Days 8 through 15

Warm-up

What better way to pursue an incremental increase in stamina than to follow the flow of rivers and canals? The territory I am navigating is blessed with three rivers and an equal number of canals. Along those waterways are tree-lined, car-free paths, wide enough to be shared by people using every possible form of metabolic energy: pedaling, running, walking, and in the case of eager children, scrambling about and tugging at their parents.

The water at our side moves ahead slowly but relentlessly, with gravity as its organic engine. Even on the slightest descent, my bicycle exploits the force of gravity. Riding and rivers have something in common.

Two thousand three hundred kilometers away, a war is raging. I have time to reflect. The ripples of the waterways seem to blend with the creases in my brain. I consider the various ways a steady state no-growth economy would reduce or even eliminate the incentives to make war.

One thing is for sure: most of the emissions-free happiness I witness along the waterways is generated outside the GDP economy.

Day 8

Funky Revelations at Both Ends of a Towpath in Epinay

Escape route number one over the Gennevilliers bridge takes me to the Epinay bridge, where the same Seine River has re-meandered. Beneath the bridge, a towpath leads both west and east with a dead end in each direction. I descend, hoping to find new paths that breach the dead ends.

Cycling west along the river, I roll by weird cliffside homes where the construction and hanging gardens are determined by the topography of the sharp bluff. The towpath then passes into a cool, woodsy dirt path, the river to the left, the wild bluff to the right. Thoreau would love the unruly chaos of both cliffside and riverbank.

The path seems to end with a freeway bridge. I walk the bike through some thick weeds and out of nowhere, a paved road appears, twisting up the bluff. This is the first steep hill I've pedaled since my operation. I look down on the pavement and just move my legs slowly. When I get near the top, on a ledge, I come upon a mélange of camper cars, likely a Romani settlement.

I see kids staring at me, the alien, while men and women do various maintenance tasks. They productively recycle stuff they've picked up from trash bins in Clichy and Gennevilliers. These travelers get a bad name for their scavenging, but it seems as if they are reducing the burden for the landfills and giving new life to old trash.

A dirt path carves into the bluff, lined with the white camper vehicles. There's broken glass on the road, so I get off and walk the bike past the campers' ledge, discovering at the top a new city: Argenteuil. On my map, it looks like dense urban sprawl. I'll check it out some other time, but it's good to know that the end of one path becomes a beginning to somewhere else.

I return to the towpath, getting off and walking the bike past the glass strewn Romani haven. They've found a place where they can remain off the radar. Even GPS will not find them.

The next part of today's leg is to retrace my path back and then cycle east on the towpath under the bridge in the direction of where the packed dirt path will suddenly end, at the border between Epinay and Saint-Denis.

I find colorful reclining chairs installed at the riverfront, white swans checking for picnic refuse, men and women pushing baby strollers, bike riders kicking up dust: more of the human big bang. At the end of the towpath, just as I am about to give up and turn around, a new portal opens before me.

Around the bend under a bridge, the towpath reopens into Saint-Denis, one of the so-called no-go zones once sensationalized on American cable television. I continue along what is now the Canal Saint-Denis. The contrast from Epinay is glaring. I see street art, graffiti art, along both sides of the canal. I've suddenly passed from peri-urban to hyper-urban, from serenity to playfulness, from edgy gardens to a former no-man's land.

I continue on the Saint-Denis towpath until glimpsing the profile of the Stade de France, the national soccer stadium. I see signs for Paris. I resolve to return another day in order to bike through the funky canal.

For the time being, I must retrace my pedal-steps. Not knowing that the Epinay towpath would open out into a new realm, I'd not brought my lunch. I return to Epinay, to a bakery with good sandwiches, grainy breads, and pastries, and to a park where I can picnic and ponder.

In his daily walks, Thoreau had sought the wild instead of the man-made. How would he have reacted to the street art along the Canal

Saint-Denis? Perhaps positively, as a manifestation of "the wild savage in us". Or he might have seen the anarchy along the canal as: "The interaction of man on man, a sort of breeding in and in…which produces a civilization destined to have a speedy limit." (281)

Day 8: 24 km. Trip to date: 134 km.

Day 9

Waterfall

The plan is to cycle to La Grande Cascade. Yes, there is a waterfall in Paris.

Henry David Thoreau died in 1862, only six years after the completion of the Bois de Boulogne in 1856 and five years before the great waterfall was added to the forest. Thoreau defended what is wild as opposed to human intervention in nature. However, he was not aware of the revolutionary advances of city planner Baron Haussmann and his daring patron, the emperor Napoleon III.

In Thoreau's writing, his opposition to the destruction of nature in the name of profit may not have contradicted with the works of Haussmann, whose parklands of the 1860s assured that the Paris of the 21st century would have a humane share of green areas. These green areas are not only in various expansive parks, but also in the smaller "squares": oases never more than a few blocks from where the pedestrian is strolling.

The Bois de Boulogne on the west side of Paris stretches out over 8.46 square kilometers, compared to the 3.41 square kilometers of Central Park in New York. Bois de Boulogne has its partner park on the east side of the city, in Bois de Vincennes: 9.95 square kilometers. To these add a half dozen other major parks within Paris, the numerous city squares, and a few Coulée Verts and you have an example of a humane urban setting.

Bois de Boulogne contains a network of cool brooks flowing lazily beneath a thick canopy. One of my favorite Boulogne bike paths runs along a brook. Yes, man-made it is, but it integrates with nature, depending less on pumps and more on geography and gravity, with the natural flow of water coming from the Canal de l'Ourcq (see Day Twenty-Six) and eastern France.

La Grande Cascade, built with rocks shipped in from Fontainebleau and with two artificial grottos sculpted by artists, still depends on the flow of nature.

So vast is the Boulogne complex that I had before me at least six or seven entirely different destinations within the park.

Today it is La Grande Cascade. I have my picnic packed and ready for a soothing visit. I anticipate finding my own Walden Pond.

When I am nearly there, I come across an obstacle. At a woodsy intersection deep within the forest, I ride by three white vans with no backside windows. In two of the driver seats are scantily-clad women whose features bulge out like hard-sell advertisements. A third woman is standing around seeming to be negotiating with a man who, annoyingly, looks like me. Another younger man is waiting by his parked car.

I imagine if I'd been Thoreau's guide in the Boulogne Forest, how he would have reacted at this aspect of human nature encroaching on the wild nature he loved. I am aware of an old truce between streetwalkers and the municipality, demanding that the sex workers vacate the city streets in exchange for allowing them to ply their trade in the woods: a romantic setting for unromantic fantasy.

Prostitutes of all sexual identities in Boulogne are often victims of violence but few lodge complaints with the police, even after a controversial 2016 law decriminalized prostitution, inscribing criminal charges against the clients. An association called *Mouvement du Nid* (Nest) defends the sex workers but opposes prostitution and has found alternative jobs for more than 800 women since 2017.

In 2018, an undocumented trans sex worker, Vanesa Campos, was shot dead in the Boulogne Forest by a gang of eight, vigilantes or robbers depending on whose version of the story is accurate. Trans prostitutes were known to work in the darkest and most remote parts of the forest.

Seven of the eight men involved in the murder were caught and sentenced, with two of them receiving the maximum of fifteen to twenty years.

Cycling away from the white van intersection, I once more immerse myself in the wounded forest. My illusions of a neo-Walden are shot, and I realize that it will be a challenge to cycle beyond the ambiguities, though I will try.

After walking on a path above the falls, watching the water roll over and looking down into the pool it creates, cradled in a grotto, I take my picnic in a pond that feeds the falls, where the illusion of a pure forest can be nurtured. Afterwards, I bicycle around to the other side of the falls for a grand panoramic view. My roundabout return route includes a stop at the *Respecte le Chêne* monument ("Respect for the Oak Tree"), a site where dozens of resistance fighters were executed by the Nazis, with traces of the bullets in the trunk of the oak, another assault on what should have been a sanctuary.

I stop to look for the bullet marks, which have since disappeared, probably because of interventions by tourists like me.

I come away from today's bike ride reminding myself that there is nowhere to escape from the ravages of the human footprint. How could I have expected otherwise, knowing that even the permafrost is no longer permanent and my favorite glacier in Bolivia has disappeared?

Day 9: 20 km. Trip to date: 154 km.

Day 10

No Cyclist Ever Rides the Same River Twice

I learned this from Heraclitus. It is not the same river, and I am not the same man. I feel much stronger today and am ready to gain more ground without taking the ever-evolving Seine for granted.

France is the luckiest country in the world when it comes to geography. It has three long seacoasts, two major mountain ranges (plus several smaller ones), and more than 100 rivers. I've done bike tours along seven of them: the Allier, the Epte, the Eure, the Loing, the Loire (Europe's wildest river), the Marne (see Day Thirty-Nine), and the Seine. None of these rivers look alike.

Some of them have brands. The Loire brand: the castles. The Seine brand: the impressionist painters.

On today's trip, I plan to pass by scenes painted by more than a dozen famous impressionists and other artists connected with the period. These include Matisse, Monet, Pissarro, Renoir, Seurat, and Sisley. I will see places where impressionist branding floods the river: Parc des Impressionnistes, Ile des Impressionnistes, and even Restaurant des Impressionnistes.

I enter the extraordinary Seine à Vélo pedestrian/bikeway just past the vast Gennevilliers shipping docks. From here on, the sailing seems as smooth on land as it is over the water. For the most part, the path is raised above the riverbank. You can look down into the water through brush and trees angling out over the water, many bending out precariously and intentionally.

At my 10 km mark, I've arrived at the Bezons bridge, my mint-and-chip destination on Day Three. Today, that destination has become a point of departure and, in the science of bicycle relativity, my sense of distance has elongated. This will be my first outing that exceeds 30 km.

On the way, there is only one climb, over an inlet bridge where I will need to lift the bike up 50 steps. The return will be more challenging: the same bridge in reverse, and then three moderately-demanding climbs between the end of the Seine bikeway and my apartment.

The big question of the day is where to stop for my picnic: a mackerel sandwich with Dijon mustard and sliced tomatoes on crusty whole-grained bread, cashew nuts, an orange, and a chocolate almond croissant, a meal that Thoreau might not have approved.

I leave today's destination to fate. At the river edge of Rueil -Malmaison, I find another Parc des Impressionnistes. It is elegant, too elegant for Thoreau. In crossing the Chatou bridge, I peer below: the Island of the Impressionists looks pretty, much like the bourgeois Sunday leisure site of Seurat's characters. Thoreau says no.

The cycle path allows me to flow with the river. I scan the surroundings for the perfect picnic spot. I keep finding faults: wrong angle of the sun, too steeply sloped for a resting place, a perfectly located bench but already occupied by a couple in love. Ultimately, it's much more fun focusing on this single decision, right now, rather than deciding on an IRA, petitioning the IRS, or wondering why our ceiling is peeling.

"What business have I in the woods," wrote Thoreau (264), "if I am thinking of something out of the woods?"

Suddenly, I arrive at a grainy stone wall to my right. Is it protecting a great secret? At an open portal, I find an apparatus with air pumps for bike tires, inviting me to stop even though I need no air.

I lift the bike up a few steps into a park with unkempt wild gardens. Three benches sit in the shade, one of them occupied by an elderly couple. They welcome me with a smile, recommending that I read the plaques about their one-of-a-kind chapel. They highlight a pointy wooden roof and below it, stonework arranged in asymmetry. Its narrow slots instead of windows identify it as a medieval fortress.

The chapel dates back to the early 11th century. Subsequent restorations have conserved certain vestiges from the original stonework. This chapel will outlive my 1970s apartment building. I plan to go in and check it out, but the shaded bench and my picnic lunch are the priority. I often imagine that a perfect picnic spot will make my lunch eternal. I eat as slowly as possible to make it so. No matter how I try to keep it going, the picnic eventually ends.

To my surprise, on this sleepy weekday afternoon, the chapel is open, and people are inside. Not impressionists, but contemporary artists in a group exposition. The chapel has become an art center. I'm especially attracted, at first, to the contrast of the colorful artwork with the grainy nooks and crannies of the stony chapel walls.

The exhibit highlights the role of humankind as an integral part of nature. How can I not think of Thoreau, who considered himself "a part and parcel of Nature, rather than a member of society" (260)?

One of the artists, Nicolas Guillemot, takes two photos and sends them to my email address. I love how he uses an ancient Japanese paper art to create a blue storm that will quiver in the wind. Since he is also a professional photographer, I can say that I have just been given two professional works of art.

It is sad that only two stray visitors have come into the chapel during my time chatting with the artists; surely in prime time, the exhibit will host larger gatherings of art lovers. I fantasize about bringing a whole tour to see the exhibit (see Day Fourteen, where this fantasy threatens to come true!).

On my return trip, inspired by Guillemot, I'm in a Japanese haiku mood.

Branches of rough bark
Elbow down, about to touch
The smooth river

I manage the three hills of my return, beginning each in what would be my normal third gear but, halfway up, shifting down to second. Never mind, I have arrived intact and with a comforting sort of fatigue.

After a half hour to chill out, I take my blood pressure. It's normal. My pulse, 65, is just fine, though five ticks above my normal of 60. Good day. Thus far I've done 198 km, nearly 20% of my objective. This was my first 30+ kilometer day. I resolve within the next week of outings to do a 40 km in this quest to prove that one can tinker incrementally with a 77-year-old body and make it stronger by cycling in a steady state.

Day 10: 36 km. Trip to date: 190 km.

Day 11

A Real Downtown: Each House Is Different, and People Walk

My destination is the idyllic Enghien racecourse. In structure, today's outing compares with the trip to the Bezons bridge ice cream stand: exactly 10 km from my front door and functioning as the day's destination even though, for later rides, it will serve as a point of departure for longer outings. Today's *parcours* resembles my earlier trip to Auteuil as Enghien racecourse was also a Hemingway hangout.

On the way, I get to use what I have labeled my In-and-Out Boulangerie, best sandwiches, pastries, and smiling service along this north suburb road.

I stick around at the track for three races, using one of their park benches (this racecourse deserves the label of parkland) for my sandwich. At the boulangerie, I'd also picked up two crusty whole-grain rye baguettes with a variety of sparkling seeds for my "campsite" dinner, but now I grab a chunk of this bread just to savor while it's fresh out of the oven.

It's a weekday so I have most of the track grounds to myself. I hang out under some towering *platane* trees (related to the sycamore) and walk over to the grandstand to make my wagers. Today, the trotters are racing: a gentler equine sport than the thoroughbreds since the legs hit the ground more softly. No bulimia is required for the harness drivers to "make the weight" and many of them look like they just came over from the farm after milking the cows.

I have the time and energy to do more than 20 km, so after the races, I explore the city of Enghien-les-Bains, a former spa with its lake large enough for small boats and its fabled theatre-casino at one edge of the water. Thoreau, even if he'd adapted to today's population sprawl, might be disappointed that the pretty lake with its swans and mallards seems to suffer from too much trimming, cutting, shaping, and maintenance.

I ride through the streets of this affluent suburban city, enjoying the contrast with the two typical California suburbs where I visit my daughters and grandson, called "cities" though they are without a downtown and without people on the streets. Here in Enghien, a real downtown thrives, the houses are markedly different from each other (not just model A, B, or C), and above all, people are walking in the streets.

"Nice place to visit," I mutter, "but too pretty to live here."

That said, there's something refreshing in seeing people get around on foot, by bicycle, and by bus or train. I'm thinking of the implicit argument of the automobile industry: "Cars don't cause fatalities, bad drivers do." Many of the same growth ideologues who lobby against gun control also lobby against proven effective measures in car control, such as building compact cities with good active transportation alternatives as I now experience viscerally in Enghien.

Example: Atlanta vs Barcelona, same population: Atlanta, car modeshare 94.9%, 564 annual traffic fatalities; Barcelona, car modeshare, 27%, 31 annual traffic fatalities. Perhaps this is one reason why I feel at ease as a "vehicular cyclist". In this territory, a critical mass of the population does not need to use a car, so the streets are more humane.

I look up above Enghien toward the forest of Montmorency, whose ponds look more like Walden than the Lac d'Enghien. For later rides, I plan to be riding deep into the hills of the vast Montmorency Forest.

On the way home, I stop off at the Parc des Sevines, my conjured-up campsite of the day. I've not had enough "exercise" today, so I enjoy the weightlifting apparatus, enveloped by springtime fragrances. The jacarandas are in full bloom. If Martha were here, we'd be debating whether they are purple or lavender in color. The name comes from the Tupi-Guaraní language of Paraguay and lowland Bolivia. It means "fragrant."

How would Thoreau greet this scene? His walking (or my cycling) "has nothing in it akin to taking exercise, as it is called, as the sick take medicine at stated hours, as the swinging of dumbbells or chairs; but is itself the enterprise and adventure of the day. If you would get exercise, go in search of the springs of life" (263).

Am I doing exercise or am I moving within the springs of life? Is this just a glorified gym or is it a fountain of colors and aromas?

Now, in my final kilometer, I roll under the shade of the classic French on-the-road trees, the *platanes*, the great, wide-trunked friends of the bike rider for the canopy they provide.

Day 11: 24 km. Trip to date: 214 km.

Day 12

Microenvironments

Finally, I have the chance to do the entire Canal Saint-Denis. I expect my *parcours* to cross three seemingly-disconnected microenvironments.

First, I must navigate the rings. The rings around Paris are as complex as the rings of Saturn, with multiple parallel paths: the annoying Périphérique freeway ring road, the outer boulevard that parallels it, the tramway whose tracks are set upon a bed of green grass within the outer boulevard, a former below-ground beltway railroad (whose empty bed is now taken over by wild gardens) and the mainly-protected bike lane. As with Saturn's rings, there will be a few turbulent gaps along the way.

The second microenvironment is the industrial funk of the Canal Saint-Denis, colorful commissioned street art, and legalized graffiti. I expect to be visually doped by all the color, and I wonder if there's some social engineering going on. By biking over the canal towpath, will I be participating in some sort of gentrification process?

My third phase begins when the canal path morphs into a car-free green corridor, a country towpath carved by the Seine, with suburban sprawl blotted out of the scenery (I had been there on Day Eight).

In all, it will be a 26 km loop.

On the bike-belt-ring path, the protected barrier provides comfort in the early going. However, on this Friday, I must elude broken glass shards on the surface from Thursday night reveling. It must get worse on the weekend.

I take a quick sideroad just before Avenue Clignancourt, lock the bike through the holes of a steel fence above the former beltway railroad bed, and descend a stairway into a wild garden with sections rented to urban farmers. I see tomatoes, grapevines, squash, and flowers of every imaginable color. There are vinelike plants framing the scene.

Back up on the bike path, I come across a delivery truck that has straddled the protective barrier, and I need to swing out into traffic to get around. Later, I wheel through a no-man's land, a massive convergence of unhoused immigrants, local homeless, and an array of street hustlers, somewhere between the Rosa Parks and Ella Fitzgerald stations of the tramway.

The path smooths out again until I arrive at the canal, descending to my left onto the sometimes dirt, sometimes paved, sometimes cobblestone pathway. I am too dazzled by the colorful artwork to pedal quickly, passing intimate parks etched into the space between the canal and the city of Saint-Denis.

The canal extends for 7 km with no two segments alike. In one short stretch, I wheel under a bridge and pass through assorted debris (I'm told that it's a "shooting gallery"), but otherwise the surface is safer than the outer boulevard bike lane.

I learn that I am cycling along "Street Art Avenue". Researchgate. net has gathered an array of studies on the transformation of Canal Saint-Denis. Some of the same researchers have published articles on urban agriculture, and this helps define the connection between the wild gardens I saw in the rings of Paris and the wild art that lines the canal.

When I began my bicycle commuting more than two decades ago, some of my gigs placed me near the sadly abandoned ring railway and the blighted Canal Saint-Denis. My before-and-after cerebral imprints highlight a vital role for playfulness in urban planning.

But will this playfulness lead to the gentrification that plagues enlightened urban areas around the world? Will real estate speculators engage in the strategy of "follow the artists"?

As the canal meets the Seine River, I wheel under a bridge into the green corridor of Epinay. The walls of legalized graffiti are gone. I share the towpath with the ubiquitous motorized scooters, slow strollers, and, here and there, a couple of lovers descending from the path to a riverside picnic bench. No one is in a hurry. I wonder how it is that they are not at work. Are they telecommuting from the park?

I'm beginning to see a bigger picture that frames the day's three microenvironments in which urban sprawl extending outward is being counteracted by rural sprawl coming in. Both the Epinay towpath and the Canal Saint-Denis function as arteries that help bring the country into the city. The urban agriculture I witnessed in the former ring railroad bed is just one image of rural sprawl being welcomed by the city.

One thing for sure: I've only begun to explore the suburban farming that may or may not be successful as sprawl tamer.

The day seems to be over before it's over as above ground crossing the bridge is Route D911 that will take me back home. I climb a ramp up to the bridge and then decide to prolong my day, carving out an alternate green alley route through parks. I zigzag through the alleys, adding both distance and pleasure, stopping for a late picnic in order to postpone the end of the ride.

I've covered three distinct but connected microenvironments, cycling through territory connected to one of the world's top three tourist cities but disconnected from the tourism circuitry.

Normally, I bump into people and strike up interesting conversations, but today I've managed to float through humanity without speaking to a soul. I look forward to Sunday, when I will be part of a group outing and once again will break the 30 km barrier.

Day 12: 26 km. Trip to date: 240 km.

Day 13

Crass Tourism, or, How Many Cities Can I Visit in One Hour?

It looks like rain for most of the day. I decide to shorten my day's outing, waiting for a break in the weather. The complete break does not arrive, so I take out the bike in a mild and almost-friendly drizzle.

Today's destination is the Olympic Village construction site on the edge of Saint-Denis. It's my first chance to sneak into the forest of towering orange cranes and see what's inside.

The Olympic Village will stand on a forgotten edge of Saint-Denis, overlooking the Seine. Some of the windows will have a good view. I think it would be easier for me to get into the Pentagon than into this Olympic Village. It is boarded up, and the best I can do is find a small space between one board and the next and stick my nose in.

The site is still in the excavation stage and, from my angle, it looks chaotic. If extraterrestrials happened to land in this place in search of advanced life, they'd prefer an ant colony to this orange forest.

This is my question: If fixing one little thing in my apartment takes an entire day, how are they going to fix this mess in time for the Olympic games two years hence?

The drizzle has subsided into an occasional droplet. I map out my game plan: cycle through eight different cities before the rain's return.

I've started in Clichy, gone through the "coastline" of our next-door-neighbor Saint-Ouen, and am now a step further down the meander of the Seine in an edge of Saint-Denis.

My definition of a city is any place that has a municipal government and a city hall. This means that Ile Saint-Denis, the island that will be seen from the windows of the Olympic Village, qualifies as a city, even if it is confined to a narrow river island.

Four minutes after I cross the bridge into Ile Saint-Denis ("hello and good-bye"), I cross over the next bridge that takes me out of Ile-Saint-Denis, and I arrive in a corner of Villeneuve-la-Garenne. I cut that corner within minutes and am now in Gennevilliers. I skirt the south edge of Gennevilliers, whose first blocks look like an industrial town from the 1940s, too gritty to call "retro," and arrive in Asnières.

That makes seven cities so far. I plan to make it eight, but this method of mine is stretching the notion of tourism. I'm not sure what's more indecent: spending only five minutes in Villeneuve-la-Garenne or spending only one night and two days in Florence as part of a package tour. Mass tourism or crass tourism?

In Asnières, I begin to feel guilty about the hyper-efficient tour I am doing, even if it must proceed as quickly as possible to beat the rain. I decide to stop in Asnières and do some bonafide tourism, parking the bike and delving into the Dog Cemetery. I applaud Asnières' tribute to the culture of 1950's US: the tomb of dog-actor Rin Tin Tin. I cannot grasp the meaning of the fact that the tomb of Rin Tin Tin may receive more visitors than the gravesite of Vincent Van Gogh and his brother Théo, my annual bicycle pilgrimage on a high plain above the pretty town of Auvers-sur-Oise.

I resist the temptation of learning about famous French dogs because the drizzle has become a mild rain, the clouds are darkening, and I have one more city to cut a corner of: Levallois.

As I ride over the Clichy bridge, the rain begins to pour down with a vengeance that can only be meant as outrage against my new brand of tourism. "Seven cities are enough," the downpour tells me.

Once over the bridge, our apartment is 200 soaking meters away.

Now back at my long-term campsite, I review the rules for the 1,000 km adventure. The "cities visited" statistic can only count cities where I have actually stopped for a visit. Tomorrow, I will be joining our local bicycle group for a tour of Le Vesinet, what some statistics list as France's wealthiest city.

Stay tuned for the "Cities Visited" statistic. I've already cut two corners out of Villenueve-La-Garenne, but it doesn't yet make the list. I plan to return to Ile Saint-Denis, a most unique island "city."

Day 13: 14 km. Trip to date: 254 km.

Day 14

Reverse Slumming and an Art Attack

I usually travel alone.

I'm not anti-social, but in a group, I am deprived of certain vital conveniences of long-distance cycling: to begin at the hour when I'm ready, to take a coffee break whenever I need to, or simply, the chance to stop and take a piss without making 20 other bicyclers wait while I find a tree.

I intend to organize a separate bike tour, *for men with prostate issues.* How's that for a niche?

However, at least twice a year, I join the wonderful picnic outings *"balades"* of MDB (*Mieux se Déplacer à Bicyclette*), the bicycle advocacy group I belong to. On Sunday, April 24, the plan is to cycle along the Seine to a sprawling park in Le Vésinet, what some surveys call the wealthiest city in France. Our ragtag group of 30-some riders are about to do some slumming in reverse. Patrick, one of the leaders, tells us we'll cycle about 35 km.

However, Le Vésinet is not far from Croissy (see Day Ten) where I had discovered the magnificent art exhibit in the quirky medieval village church, La Chapelle de Saint-Leonard. If you recall, I loved the group exhibit, Nature in Art: the Place of Humans Among Living Things, based on the concept that we human beings are an integral part of nature.

The artworks were compelling and inspiring, but I had been saddened that the seven artists were relegated to waiting around for an occasional stray visitor. I'd not arrived at prime time, so surely there were more visitors at other hours.

Before the outing, I suggest to Patrick that we do a quick side trip to the Croissy exhibit. He agrees, but he does not let everyone know until after we are riding.

I fear that some of the participants might be grumbling, either because they did not care for art exhibits or that they have not bargained to go beyond 35 km. They might be grumbling against me, since Patrick has told them it was my idea.

Thank you, Patrick, for putting me, a loner, on the spot.

And what if, after the extra pedaling, we are not particularly welcomed in the tight quarters of the chapel? After all, we do not look like a gang of art collectors.

After Patrick announces our detour, following a splendid picnic in the manicured Le Vésinet park and a gawking tour of the elegant mansions, some two-wheel negotiating is taking place. Everything is set up for me to be perceived as the annoyance of the day. Two or three of our group leave to go home. I feel the pressure is on me.

But to my surprise, most, even the seniors of the seniors, delight in the extra adventure. There are a few artists among us, including Anabel, a Spanish composer-singer-guitarist (she and her husband had recently cycled from Paris to London via the Dieppe ferry). We arrive at the church on the last day of the exhibit. I've assumed that Sunday is prime time for such an event. Yet, as the group locks their bikes outside the chapel, I peek inside. There is only a single visitor.

I tell the elegant Aurélia, the artist *animatrice,* a figure Modigliani would have loved, that I've brought some visitors. Little does she know that there are more than two dozen of them. I wonder if she will feel overwhelmed, in the negative sense, since the riffraff has arrived. A single authentic art buyer is worth more than a horde of platonic viewers.

I suspect, though, she'll be thrilled. On my previous visit, she'd said, in near-perfect English, that "I aim to break the conformism of society by confronting it to a new reality that requires the participation of humans, as viewers, participants or models, and as an essential condition for the realization of a work."

As we file in, her eyes light up. She assumes the role of gracious host, giving concise but thoughtful explanations of the work of each of the artists. From the nuanced questions posed by some of our biking companions, it becomes apparent that we are not the riffraff after all.Once the show is done and my companions have left the chapel, Aurèlia invites me to stick around for the post-exhibit wine celebration. I'm tempted. I savor the idea of an early evening tipsy bike ride for some 18 km along the wooded banks of the Seine, where no cars will threaten and where it was not prohibited for bicyclers to drink and drive.

After having taken my companions out of their way, and in a few cases probably against their will, it seems wrong to ditch them. I politely decline the invite.

As explained in the Day Ten chapter, Croissy-sur-Seine is a town of much history. I hope that our art attack will become a minor, but worthy, moment in that history.

I later learn that the exhibit has been extended for an extra week. I would love to believe that our horde of attendees played some role in the extension of the exhibit, but that's surely not the case. Aurélia Bizouard and her colleagues are international artists of great prestige. The artists themselves have done a favor to take their works to a small town, far removed from the Parisian art scene where they are well-known and thriving.

Day 14: 40 km. Trip to date: 294 km.

Day 15

Trail of Two Cities

I wake up after the previous day's art incursion with my back threatening to give out.

I decide not to take a day off but to lower my expectations. I take the three aspirins that usually zap the back threat (not medical advice!) and put on a back brace to ease me back to normal.

My reduced plan is for island hopping, selecting two islands that seem to be following each other in the parade of 117 surviving islands in the 482-mile Seine River.

My sociology tour involves a compare-and-contrast essay question. I've been to both islands but in doing them back-to-back, I anticipate learning something new.

Island 1: Ile-de-Jatte lies across the river as part of two adjacent cities, Neully-sur-Seine, the second wealthiest city in France, and affluent Levallois, famous for a multiple-term mayor who ended up in prison after being convicted of corruption.

Island 2: Ile-de-Saint Denis has its own city hall but is overshadowed by the city of Saint-Denis, the 8th or the 16th poorest city in all of France, depending on the source of the research. Ile-Saint-Denis has a 33% poverty rate while Ile-de-Jatte has a much lower percentage of poverty than the cities it is part of, and in fact, there may not be a single poor person on the Ile-de-Jatte oasis.

This is not a recent phenomenon, as the pointillist painter Georges Seurat *pointed out* in his famous "A Sunday Afternoon on the Grand Jatte" (1884), which took two years to paint/point. The Simpsons did a parody of the Seurat painting, which in effect was a parody of the parody, for Seurat was commenting on the artificiality of modern Parisian society. Ile-de-Jatte was their hangout.

It's a pretty bike ride, end to end, of Ile-de-Jatte, with a separate bike path on either edge. On the banks of the river, a parade of funky-ostentatious houseboats captures the imagination, as if they were floats at the Rose Parade. Aside from its parks, stately homes, condominiums, and elegant restaurants, the island has rows of tennis courts. Above all, it is a wooded oasis with twisting paths and a few mild hills, so it makes for an attractive bike ride.

However, there are frequent stops as the island features tableau-copies of different impressionist painters, including Seurat. Each copy of a painting is situated exactly where it was originally done, pointing in the direction that the painter was facing at the time.

The west end of the island is shaped like a finger pointing, beyond the river, at the emblematic La Défense business, shopping, and entertainment district: once modernist architecture, fallen in disfavor, and today in recovery and rediscovering itself with landscape architecture and a ramblas type public hangout along the esplanade.

Once leaving Ile-de-Jatte, I take a wooded bike path half the way east toward Ile-Saint-Denis. The path morphs into an industrial zone where the car traffic is fast and furious, and where, in the absence of a bike path, I take the uneven sidewalk. I pass by old graffiti at an industrial wasteland, where nature is clawing its way back through a condemned building.

A profusely overgrown "penthouse" hangs out from the third and top floor, where no human being partakes of the wild. The graffiti on the bottom floor surface cannot compete in sophistication with spray can art along Canal Saint-Denis. However, it does once more establish the connection between wild gardens and wild art.

I arrive at a modern housing development/park called Les Docks in Saint-Ouen, where I notice muskrats swimming in the pond. In *Walden*, Thoreau has referred to muskrats, but here these critters are considered an invasive species. Up front, they look cute like a beaver but from behind, their rat's tail ruins the scene. I see a Canadian goose flap at a muskrat, as if to say, "get off my turf", and the muskrat scrambles away.

I cross the bridge on to Ile-Saint-Denis. It's a weird place. From above, it looks like a long fish with the tail end an industrial zone and the front end a pretty park with attractive hills and paths, reminding me of the ambiguous muskrat.

Between the two ends of the island is a single cross-street downtown with a small city hall. This is very much a working-class city, even if a modest attempt at gentrification has installed some colorful apartment buildings at the tail end. The old industrial section has seen better days and seems slated to crumble away. Nature encroaches amidst the rubble.

Now, what can I write on my compare-and-contrast essay, after having ridden a total of only 14 km? On my scoreboard, I no longer saw the rats that used to scamper across Ile-de-Jatte, and Ile-Saint-Denis also seems free from those pesky Parisian invaders.

The leftovers from elegant Ile-de-Jatte restaurants may be tastier than the main dishes on Ile-Saint-Denis.

I felt as if I were whiffing fertilizer in a beautiful Ile-de-Jatte garden whereas wild vegetation along the industrial edge of Ile-Saint-Denis thrives on its own, even if I find a few beer cans and candy wrappers in the bushes, as well as a broken bottle or two right in the middle of a faded old bike lane that's hardly recognizable.

As for wildlife, on Ile-de-Jatte I've never seen such a population density of dog walkers, with some dog owners allowing their pets to swim in the Seine. In the park area of Ile-Saint-Denis, I find jackrabbits, and the magpies seem to have learned from those rabbit neighbors to hop around. The dogs might be happier in the Parc Ile-Saint-Denis, with more extensive space to jump and run in.

As I would learn in subsequent bike rides, municipalities along the Seine are all in competition to name their parks and islands "*Impression-istes*". Even my hometown of Clichy has one of those.

If I were a consultant for Ile-Saint-Denis, on the other hand, I'd suggest they invite industrial wasteland photographers such as Robert Brook and Patrick Landmann to have a go at it before the post-industrial half of the island cedes to the forces of gentrification.

Day 15: 14 km. Trip to date: 308 km.

Third Movement: Forest Therapies

Days 16 through 26

Warm-up

As I ride deeper into the shady woodlands in the region surrounding Paris, recall that the idea of Thoreau on a bike is supposed to encourage the healthy, joyful, and zero-emissions activity of metabolic travel anywhere in the world, including within the USA, where I have my roots.

France has a superb record of reforestation, especially following the devastating Christmas storm of 1999, which we witnessed in fright. That violent storm took down a million hectares of forest.

Thirty-six American states exceed the admirable 31 percent forest coverage of France. For example, more than 60% of Thoreau's Massachusetts is graced with woodlands. Even the urbanized District of Columbia has a slightly higher percentage of forest cover than France. Americans reading these pages need not fly to France to follow the Thoreau template for travel by bicycle or on foot, especially if they are from Maine, whose forests cover nearly 90 percent of its territory.

This is not to downgrade France's forests, especially in the realm of accessibility. Many French cities have little or no suburban sprawl separating them from the nearest woodlands. The city of Compiègne, for example, is nestled within a major forest. Furthermore, at least 8,000 kilometers of cycling paths cross through French forests, as well as 11,000 km of walking paths.

I'm now ready to cycle into more of the woodlands outside of Paris, with no preconceptions of what I will find.

Day 16

Landslide Forest: "No IKEA What's Going On!"

In this third movement of the 1,000 km, I'm looking into forests to complement the river therapies of the previous movement. I've seen Bois des Eboulures on my map and roughly translated it to the Forest of Landslides. The weird name of this place makes it worthy of a visit, and it will give me yet another plus-30-km day.

On the map, Route D14 looks like sprawl, but I'm ready for surprises. Halfway between Epinay and Bois des Eboulures, D14 is marked on my map as having a bike path, and if you believe that a bike path is faded paint, then you got it. In the segments with no bike path, the road cycling is smooth as I have no encounters with impatient car drivers.

The towns along D14 are skirting a wooded hill, steep enough to keep out the speculator riffraff. From time to time, I leave D14 and venture to my left to get a glimpse of the foothills. I find winding streets with classic shuttered town houses, and I find endings to the towns. Well-delineated endings make for great towns. The extended wooded hill acts as a fortress against suburban sprawl.

Some of these attractive departure roads tempt me to abandon the destination of Bois des Eboulures and go exploring, but I'm driven to find out what Eboulures is all about.

It becomes more intriguing when a half-dozen different locals I've consulted seem unaware of which is the cutoff route that will take me into these woods. They all give friendly guesses; this solidarity is based on shared obliviousness.

No one seems to have visited Bois des Eboulures.

It gets more intriguing when I do an informal survey on "What is an *Eboulure*?" Each of the six locals I survey have no idea of what it is or what it means. I wonder with excitement if I will be the first human being to ever visit the Bois des Eboulures.

At one point, I am tempted to give up. In the distance, instead of a forest, I see a giant box, blue and yellow, which has encrusted itself into the wooded hill along the road. Someone has played a joke on me, sacrificing a chunk of woods for rude geometry. Could it be a hangar for an experimental UFO? Or the protective covering of a waste recycling plant? No way. A waste removal plant would be washed in green, not blue and yellow. Or maybe this is Bois des Eboulures, walled in to stop a further landslide. Maybe that big box is the missing definition of "*eboulure*".

I roll up in front of the box, brake, and now identify the logo. It is IKEA, with all the false wood inside replacing the real wood outside. GrowthBusters would probably point to the ugly big box obscenely etched into the wooded hill and remind us that we cannot ignore the impacts of population growth. Less and less space is available to fulfill the needs of more and more people in exurban Paris.

Across the road from IKEA is a parking lot, the type that Sprawl Busters would be opposing. After all my cycling trips outside of Paris, I have finally found an American suburb (Sprawl Busters is headquartered only 70 miles from Walden Pond)!

Yet my map shows the forest to be at this spot. I cycle through the parking lot, and there it is, hidden behind the big boxes.

With no help from the friendly locals, who may never have seen this forest because of the cement veil in front of it, I've found the Bois with a literal interpretation of my contour map.

Upon entering the woods, I seem to be the only visitor. I look for a tree stump to sit and picnic. For my lunch, I've scraped up any old slices of grainy bread, pieces of goat cheese, cherry tomatoes, cucumber slices, and olives. I did not even make a sandwich. I threw in some cashews to the mix. This picnic lunch remains simple: no Dijon this time, no other spread to enhance the flavor, and only water to wash it down. Thoreau would approve.

I have not been able to find the quote from Hesse's *Narcissus and Goldmund* where Goldmund declares that he'd rather eat this crusty old bread in the mountains than dine with the guildsmen in town, but this is exactly the way I feel, as I breath the fresh spring aromas of the forest and wait for some other member of my species to show up.

I have no IKEA what's going on here! The Bois des Eboulures is located in the suburban city of Franconville, at the edge of that high forested cliff. In the meditative silence of these woods, my thoughts finally come upon the reason for IKEA's blue and yellow, something like, "Yes, I am not green, screw you."

Or maybe the opposite is true, with IKEA concocting a primeval form of green, retaining the blue and yellow before they mixed and evolved into green. Meditating on IKEA gets me no closer to finding the meaning of *"eboulures"*.

According to one local newspaper, authorities have no idea where the name *"eboulures"* comes from, and the geological definition of the word is much more nuanced than my "landslide" definition. It has something to do with unstable land.

This site was heavily impacted by the famous 1999 Christmas Eve storm which Martha and I experienced back in Paris. During that storm, 1,200 trees were felled in the Bois des Eboulures. The story here is how forests can regenerate, with the help of human beings, the ones I am still looking for. This is an example of our species restoring the earth instead of destroying it and could be used as a model for the future. I find no signs of the 1999 destruction as I sit on this irregular stump and finish off my picnic, cheese chunk by cheese chunk, cashew by cashew. My strategy for slowing down the big bang universe expansion is one nut at a time.

Later, as I tour the woods, I come upon a lake, and with it, people. A woman walking a baby in a stroller with two bare chubby feet sticking out. Two men sitting on a bench and drinking something that looks better than the water I just consumed. From the distance, I spot a giant grey heron in the middle of the lake.

To get a clearer view, I leave my bike and step through thick undergrowth that has not been shaved down by park custodians. Soon, I realize that the giant heron is a sculpture. I wonder what the real grey heron will think when he sees a statue of himself. I suspect that Thoreau would say: "Methinks why make a statue of nature in the middle of nature herself?"

I flee back into the woods to the same picnic stump and meditate before my long ride back to the old hearth. Once back on the road, cycling in the reverse direction from whence I came, everything looks fresh and new with the opposite perspective. I enjoy the ups and downs and the ins and outs along the way.

I've left behind the chain stores, and now the local Ma-and-Pa commerce decorates my route. Most Parisian suburbs seem to be resisting the extremes of sprawl, but some of this resistance is a cover-up. From cycling on other roads, I've barely noted that big box shopping center parking lots will hide behind ivy walls, as if there were a "No Overt Soliciting" ordinance.

Some French town planners seem embarrassed by parking lot ugliness, while in the USA, there's no shame about airing dirty laundry along a sidewalk.

For the moment, I am happy to cycle on a road that is not lined by parking lot blight. The only thing I am missing is a tee-shirt with the word *EBOULURES* emblazoned on my chest.

Day 16: 32 km. Trip to date: 340 km.

Day 17

City Farmers in Montmagny

The city of Epinay is becoming a regular departure point. The next city to the north, Montmagny, presents opportunities for the bike explorer. For a useful perspective, Montmagny in France has a population density of nearly 5,000 inhabitants per square kilometer, while the population density of Montmagny in Quebec is 1,350 people per square kilometer. My city of Clichy has nearly 20,000 inhabitants per square kilometer, compared to 28,000 for Manhattan.

I am here to explore the works of art of the local city farmers and get a feel for the balance between density and farming.

Throughout the city, on east and west sides, are *ruelles*, narrow passageways lined with gardens, some of which are large enough to be considered small farms. I explore these *ruelles* slowly, encountering from time to time the gardeners themselves.

One gardener sends a smile while another glances up at me, seeming to wonder what I am doing there, as if I were encroaching. These *ruelles* are considered streets, each with a name, but they come into such close proximity with people's homes that I feel I'm about to invade someone's backyard barbeque.

Some of the *ruelles* skirt cool woods, a few have large panoramas, while the ones that spy into backyards make for an awkward ride.

I reflect on one potential statistic. What if only 20% of the millions of back or front yard lawns in the USA were converted to gardening for produce? What would the impact be on the environment?

The benefits are well documented. Plants take in CO_2. Roots benefit the soil. Locally grown produce means fewer trips to the food market, fewer chemical inputs, and less of the perverse produce travel distances from farm to market. Composting reduces waste disposal. Gardening adds natural habitats that have been disappearing.

Could Montmagny's network of *ruelles* be a model for the transformation of American suburbs? Could it alleviate the wounded habitat in territory outside of Paris?

Once I finish zigzagging through the *ruelles*, I go into the city hall and ask if I can fill up my water bottle. The attendant obliges with a smile and hands me some pamphlets. She recommends the Butte Pinson, whose forest hides an ecological farm called, appropriately, *La Ferme*. But *La Ferme* is only open to the public on weekends. I make a mental note to return on a Saturday or Sunday, planning to cycle directly into the hillside forest to reach this ecological and educational farm.

The retro road down from the Montmagny city hall on the way to Epinay is energizing as the scene resembles a classic French village: connected townhouses with façades of rough textures and colorful window shutters. There is only one lane.

I weave around traffic-calming devices. An occasional car driver behind me slows down without honking. Attitudes of local car drivers toward bike riders have largely evolved from impatience, twenty years ago, to respect. I share this respect by moving over when the lane gets wide enough for a car to pass.

Many of my French friends and acquaintances have parents or grandparents who were farmers. Could Montmagny be a shining green example of rural sprawl or is it a mere outlier? I will try to find out.

Day 17: 20 km. Trip to date: 360 km.

Day 18

UV and SUV Warnings

When the going gets hot and tough, I search for the sweet and soft solution. My maps are open on the dining room table, and I attempt to plot out a route that will be fully protected by the tree canopy. I am taking no chance with the UV warnings.

I'm on my way. I've got the full shade on the protected bike lanes through the "coastal" route of Levallois. This paradise ends where Neuilly begins, but from here I take a street with broad sidewalks and enormous trees lining the way. No surprise that Neuilly is the Beverly Hills of France; its citizens are coddled by leafy green boulevards.

(The best bicycle I'd ever owned, a black Dutch bike with 28-inch tires, was stolen from a Neuilly street. I'd locked it to an iron fence, then entered a building for an hour gig. I left the building whistling a song, feeling good from the espresso coffee they had served me. Then I saw it. In the empty space where my bike should have been, the thieves left me a souvenir, the perfectly sawed-off lock, gleaming in the sun. Later, the policeman taking my report seemed in awe at the professionalism of those bike thieves.)

This Neuilly street ends on a T-junction at a food store. The neighbors standing outside the shop wonder why I am so meticulous in locking my bike in their crime-free haven just to go in and pick up sandwiches, nuts, and a chocolate bar for dessert. Around the corner, I tackle the sun for only two blocks until I enter the Boulogne Forest. I zigzag through the forest until I come out at my Existential Intersection.

Another city is upon me: Boulogne-Billancourt. But what about the UV warnings? Do I retreat into the forest, or move forward? I love this dilemma because it fully occupies my thoughts, taking my mind off the larger worries, which I leave for op-ed pundits, who will get paid, right or wrong. What would Thomas Friedman decide in my place? I bet that all those pundits who boldly hyped a preventive war in Iraq, would, if facing my Existential Intersection, recommend a preventive retreat into the forest.

My feeling is the opposite. It is bad to invade sovereign countries but good to invade the sovereign city of Boulogne-Billancourt, even with the UV warnings. Tree cover is sporadic, but I do get the afternoon shade from six-floor buildings lining the west side of the avenue. I've added sunblock and am ready to encroach.

I will have to confront SUVs, the modern-day tanks that increasingly crowd the cramped spaces of affluent Boulogne-Billancourt. One can shield against UVs, but some climate scientists say that SUVs are weapons of mass destruction. I have one mission and one destination.

Mission: Boulogne-Billancourt is the gateway for the seignorial Parc Saint-Cloud, which, in turn, is a gateway for Versailles. I scout the streets for the best way to get to the sprawling, multi-level Parc Saint-Cloud, find it, and make a mental note for a later ride. Boulogne-Billancourt is now fully navigable for me, and even the ubiquitous SUVs cannot stop me.

Destination: For now, I'm back on a main street, and I will declare victory when I reach the Museum-Garden Albert Kahn. I've been to this garden on several occasions and have enjoyed the playful imagination of the multiple landscapes within, which imitate French, English, Japanese, wild prairie, and forest gardens. I would have wanted to take my picnic inside, but a long line is waiting beneath the unforgiving sun.

I practice guerrilla tactics, knowing when to attack and when to retreat. It is worse to be standing immobile under the intense sunlight than riding through it. I hop on my bike and take a different route back to the forest. My reconnaissance mission has been successful. I've survived the UVs and the SUVs.

A slow and glorious picnic awaits on a shaded bench next to a brook. Thanks to my geographic preparation, any sunrays I may confront on the way home will hit me from behind.

Day 18: 26 km. Trip to date: 386 km.

Day 19

Lost in the Woods

Yesterday's reconnaissance in Boulogne-Billancourt has pointed the way to one of my favorite places. I must cross over the river into the expansive Parc de Saint-Cloud, do a long climb past the residence of Marie-Antoinette, and pass through the woods to Ville d'Auvray to relax at the ponds made famous by the painter Corot.

It's hotter than yesterday but knowing the exact streets through Boulogne-Billancourt is a time saver. Crossing the Seine at this juncture is a puzzle to be solved as I must find the path that goes either over or under an annoying freeway on the other side of the river. This is the worst time to navigate through "Cementville", but I locate a bike lane that is mostly hidden from view, and it takes me down a slope to a park entrance.

It is here where I commit the original sin. The paths to Ville d'Auvray are on the left side of the park. The multi-leveled climb has taken me to the right side of the park. It looks much the same, so I assume this wooded pedestrian boulevard will take me to where I need to go.

After riding for a longer time than it once took me to walk, I realize that I am going in the wrong direction. My sense of direction tells me to go left, but by the time I do (which I will later find out), I am already past the exit to Ville d'Auvray.

I am so beaten down by the heat that I wonder how I will ever get back home. I am at an exit at the opposite end of the park where I need to be. The guard at the gate gives me a map of the entire forest. He looks like he's from Bolivia, and when I ask him in Spanish, I recognize his Andean accent. He's from Perú, which is almost like being home for me, so the conversation distracts me from my fatigue.

I want desperately to notch in the 13th city of my 1,000 km odyssey, but Marnes-la-Coquette, pretty as it looks, does not count because I am not stopping here.

I've crossed a 460-hectare forest (1,137 acres), designed by Le Notre for the brother of Louis XIV, and seen some awesome views of Paris from the high bluff above the fountains. I have one incentive to beat my fatigue: a stop at an ice cream vendor in the Boulogne Forest, about halfway home, where the pistachio ice cream is unbeatable.

The anticipated ice cream break motivates me to overcome the heat and get through Boulogne-Billancourt.

When I get the Bois de Boulogne lakeside snack stand, I discover they are out of pistachio, and they do not even have mint-and-chip. This leads to yet another existential decision. Do I settle for any old flavor and make believe it's pistachio, or do I pass?

While this dilemma is occupying my mind and soul, I have not thought for a second about the war in Ukraine, not thought about all the birds that are crashing into eolian windmills and plunging to their death, not thought about the allergy that has attacked my beloved wife during her stay in Bolivia, not thought about the fact that I had recently forgotten the name of my blood pressure medication, which I have been taking for two decades, only to remember the name a half hour after I'd left the office of the doctor who had asked me about my medications.

I have forgotten that at 77 years old, I may only have a few years or a few days left on this earth.

The only thing I have on my mind is the need for one damn scoop of ice cream to help me beat this fatigue. I decide not to settle for any old ice cream, and that I will search for another stand along the way.

As I leave the forest and cycle through the shady streets of Neuilly, the fatigue has dissipated. I am well again and worried about my wife. Instead of looking for the ice cream, I pedal home, full speed ahead, to call her.

Day 19: 38 km. Trip to date: 424 km.

Day 20

Celebrating My Day of Ignorance

It was May 1st, a day of great symbolism for me since it exposed my penchant for ignorance. I was 19 years old, hitchhiking across Latin America, waiting for a ride on a rural stretch of road in El Salvador. I held up a sign: *Gringo al Sur* (Gringo to the South).

The sign was not working its usual magic as I'd been waiting for longer than usual under the tropical sun. A peasant in sandals walked up to me, shook my hand, and congratulated me. I had no idea why.

"This is your day to celebrate," he said. "The First of May!"

I must have looked perplexed as I asked him to specify.

"The martyrs of Chicago!"

I was too embarrassed to ask for an American history lesson from a poor peasant in El Salvador, so I waited until my return to the States.

Back in the USA, I looked up the First of May in the library, got the basics, then sought out a professor of labor history, asking him how was it that I had been ignorant of the 1886 Haymarket Square massacre. He explained that there had been an organized effort on the part of American leaders to make us forget about that symbolic period in American history when workers were fighting for the eight-hour workday. The history of protest was excluded from the curriculum when I went through the public schools, and the event knew no national celebration in the USA, even though it was a holiday in the rest of the world. Today I see an equivalence as the Chinese Communist Party attempts to bury the events of Tiananmen Square from the collective memory of the Chinese people. As a result, I attend May 1st marches in Paris to remind myself that I am prone to ignorance and can benefit from collective celebrations of history.

I have a second reason to shout "present" as two French labor unions backed our protest as adjunct professors who were working without contracts at the prestigious school of higher education, Sciences Po. Among our laundry list of grievances, we were fighting against a national mandatory retirement age. Thanks to our union membership, we won three extra years of work eligibility.

It's only 8 km from my apartment to Place de la République, the gathering place for the march. For my return, I plan on taking a round-about trip along two canals I've not yet cycled during my intended 1,000 km voyage: Canal Saint-Martin through the east of Paris and Canal de l'Ourcq, which stretches through the northeast suburbs and beyond.

My trip to République involves bike lanes carved within sidewalks on two major boulevards, where the bicycle rider needs to watch for stray pedestrians and broken glass on the path. I view these lanes as a temporary fix to the larger problem of too much space for cars and not enough for pedestrians and bike riders. Squeezing in bike lanes needs to be accompanied by squeezing out cars, but for the latter to take place, an expanded menu of comfortable transportation alternatives needs to be available to car drivers.

At the march, I say hello to a few people I know, including a friend who had been sharing info on her PhD thesis in art history. She can eyeball any building and sketch out its history. I end up marching with another group that you will meet in a later episode of this chronicle, but for the time being, I can say that after having spotted potential *agents provocateurs* I decide to leave the march of twenty thousand and be on my way.

Along the canals are hundreds of thousands of revelers hanging out and celebrating the First of May. If 10% of them had joined the march, the French labor movement would have had far greater leverage. I stop at one bend in the Canal Saint-Martin where the smooth surface of the water is, remarkably, higher than the surface of the street.

Construction of the canal was ordered by Napoleon in 1802 and began in 1825 thanks to funding from a wine tax. The canal brought fresh water into the city as well as grain and cement shipments. Wine for water seemed like a good trade-off. Thanks to public protest, the canal survived a brutalist 1970's attempt at replacement with a freeway. It's a magical sight with its venetian-style bridges and Panama style locks. My favorite retro view of the canal is in Alfred Sisley's 1870 painting *View of the Canal Saint-Martin*, which hangs in the Orsay Museum.

I get lucky this time around, getting to see a cruise boat passing through one of the locks; only a few meters separate me from the passengers. For a moment, I'm tempted to have a slow beer at an outside table at Chez Prune and do nothing for the rest of the afternoon, but I need to rack up kilometers, and it's a splendid day to pedal around. I take my northerly suburban route, enjoying the beginning of Canal de l'Ourcq but saving that canal for a longer trip. I wheel back to Clichy, with 30 km added to my *carnet de voyage*.

For May 2nd, I will shoot for 50 km for an extended May Day celebration, which would take me beyond the 500 km barrier.

Day 20: 30 km. Trip to date: 454 km.

Day 21

Reality Tour: From Impressionism to Expressionism

My destination is a hilly part of the Seine, a town called Le Port Marly. Years back, I'd tried to reach Le Port Marly but was thwarted by a stretch of obscene traffic with no alternate route. This time, I intend to walk the bike past any difficult stretch I encounter. The scenery of steep wooded hills is too beautiful to miss. It is not made for the presence of speeding cars.

This is the same riverside route whose new symbolic "departure" is under the Bezons Bridge. For the sake of diversity, I arrive at that point on the Seine River by taking a less protected but new route through the suburbs of Courbevoie and La Garenne-Colombes, briefly getting lost along the way.

It's a cloudy afternoon and I now understand how this stretch of the Seine was a high activity zone for the impressionist painters. The skies are often threatening, but there is rarely a storm, so the painter gets to see all kinds of textural variation.

I feel particularly strong today, highly motivated in anticipation of my first 50 km day in this daily sequence of expeditions. However, as the riverside becomes attractively hillier, the clouds become more menacing.

At an outdoor toilet structure in Rueil-Malmaison, I ask a woman who is holding her cell phone if she has an updated weather forecast.

"I hope you don't become drenched," she responds. "There's an 80 percent chance of thunderstorms."

Passing under the Chatou Bridge, the bikeway is now shared with an occasional car but is entirely safe thanks to traffic calming promontories. Then the road ends, the surface becomes packed dirt, and the clouds get darker. I detour for a short kilometer into the edge of a forest. Once back on the river path, I stop for an impressive view of the hills. I should say "expressive view" since the skies are more befitting of an impassioned expressionist painting of Edvard Munch than a Monet.

I get to the "coast" of Bougival and would love to cycle up the steep hill of this pretty town and step into the towering gothic church before proceeding on to Port Marly. However, as I stop the bike behind the former home of composer Georges Bizet on a gravelly section lined with blooming flowers, I feel a raindrop touch my right ear and then another one on my left hand. I don't mind five or six kilometers in the rain, but my "campsite" is now too far for a ride in the rain in thunderstorms.

I'm confronted again with an existential decision. If I turn back from here, I will be so near and yet so far from my 50 km day and even nearer to the church on the hill, now framed with dark storm clouds.

I decide to turn back and not be influenced by an arbitrary number. I go through a brief drizzle, pressing on to beat the thunder and lightning. Once I have reached the exit from the Seine à Vélo, a mere 8 km from home, the sun comes out. I can affirm, after the fact, that I made the wrong decision.

However, the threat of rain has given me a good workout. This is the fastest I've pedaled for the entire 496 kilometers. Yes, I will arrive home short of the 500, but with a wonderous fatigue that can only be felt after a perfect workout.

Day 21: 42 km. Trip to date: 496 km.

Day 22

The Peppertree and the 15-Minute City

With my daily outings taking up much of my time, my mundane tasks have been accumulating. Whatever I do, wherever I go, today I will pass the 500 km milestone, so why not piece together a multiple-task catch-up day into a bike ride?

My goal has been to create the illusion of a long-distance bike tour, but I fear that I will find no imaginative crossroad between the day's utilitarian outing and the Big Journey. I struggle with how to make this day a continuity rather than a rupture from my voyage with Thoreau.

I am planning four different destinations. Books and magazines slated for the book share bins have been accumulating, and without new material to read myself to sleep, my mind has been playing the worry game and sleep disorder has set in. The "little free library" or "book box" in the Levallois botanical garden seems like a good place to do an exchange. I pack what I have to offer in my backpack.

My compost has been overflowing, so I need to unload. I put the compost in the bike's basket. The book exchange and the compost center seem like two sectors of a non-growth steady state economy.

I've gone too long without a lifting workout, so once I've unloaded the books and compost, I can cycle to Parc des Sevines to use the lifting apparatus. This is a fitness center with no exchange of money involved, which means it plays a minimal role in the GDP economy but a maximal role for the health of the citizens.

Once finished in Parc des Sevines, I will be near Villeneuve-la-Garenne, a city that has not yet been added to my "cities visited" score and there's a story taking place that is worth checking out, with the Caravelle neighborhood having gone two years without a supermarket to replace the departed Lidl chain. I've seen articles that suggest it's a food desert, so as a student of urban quality of life, I want to see for myself.

I improvise a change in plan, making the compost dump my first stage. Unloading the potent blend will be therapeutic. When I open the box in Parc des Impressionistes, all kinds of insects fly up into my face, a sign that the composting is doing its job. I dump and jump, on to the next task.

At the book bin in the botanical garden, in the next town down the road, I unload a few books and scan what's available in exchange. I find a novel, in English, called *Trial* by Clifford Irving, which is said to be a page turner. I also find a newspaper with an unsolved crossword puzzle. I've been doing French crosswords, with the idea that I can establish new neural connections to stave off whatever has been happening to the mind in old age. Both the novel and the crossword will divert my bedtime thoughts away from senseless worrying.

I am about to leave the garden when something tells me, "Not so fast!" Belatedly, I remember that I am surrounded by trees and plants from around the world. What better place to linger than under the Bolivian *molle* (moyaye) tree. The leaves of the *molle*, hanging from gnarly branches, are pungent and even tangy like a mild chili pepper. No wonder it's called a peppertree.

During my cycling in Bolivia, my favorite rest stop was under a *molle* tree. Of the five senses, the sense of smell is most powerful in evoking memories. I find a bench under this Bolivian tree, take a fernlike leaf cluster, rub the leaves in front of my nostrils, and breathe in the cool spiciness. I am now on the road, taking a break, and conjuring up the EPO effects from high altitude cycling.

I consider just hanging out here and doing the rest of my planned trip at another time. But I can take my tiny cluster of peppertree leaves with me to Parc des Sevines. This is what I would do in La Paz, where a cluster of *molle* trees was near to my exercise park in Achumani.

The two-sided lifting apparatus in Parc des Sevines is vacant. It has the same design as the one I used in Bolivia. I do my lifting, armed with the aroma of the peppertree. I do my best to stop thinking. My mantra is an aroma. I could be in the northern hemisphere or the southern hemisphere.

Finally, I stop lifting and land in the northern hemisphere. It's time for Villeneuve-la-Garenne, a working-class city of 25,000 inhabitants with a bulging demographic for the age 0 to 14 population. I get there through Parc des Chanteraines. I will use my own food shopping to identify the potential food desert.

In effect, the site for the replacement supermarket is still in preparation. Intermarché will be the new food supplier. I find smaller Ma-and-Pa groceries as well as a Carrefour supermarket outside the targeted neighborhood but still within what Martha and I consider shopping-walking distance.

Since I've been out of bread, I purchase two multi-cereal baguettes in a well-stocked bakery, and sucker that I am, add a pistachio pastry because it's hard to find, even in Paris. I see no threat of a potential food desert but the folks who live in the Caravelle housing project deserve their supermarket. This will help with a perceived goal of a "15-minute city," a place where everything is within strategic walking distance.

It's been a cool and sparkling day to promote utilitarian bicycling as if it were the "enterprise and adventure of the day" (263). I've added a name to my cities-visited list.

Big day coming, a visit to the underrated garden city of Taverny.

Day 22: 30 km. Trip to date: 526 km.

Day 23

Taverny *Sentes*

On my annual bike pilgrimages to Vincent Van Gogh's grave in Auvers-sur-Oise, I used to pass through Taverny without making a stop. I knew I was missing something. The day has now arrived when I can explore Taverny's side streets and its east edge slope along the Montmorency Forest.

I decide not to become discouraged by the city hall, which looms into my view as either the product of deranged '70s architecture or of science fiction novels conjuring up a structure built by extraterrestrials. This one structure is a scar on what is otherwise a well-preserved French townscape.

To get here, I've gone through Enghien and then up Route D928. I could have chosen a parallel bike path a couple of blocks away, but sharing this D928 with car traffic is without the least stress.

Just past the city hall, I turn right up into the hills. As it gets steeper, it looks like I will have to get off and push, but to my right, I find a narrow dirt-packed garden path with a gentler slope. I'm drawn in by the colors and aromas of what we call "nature," and I turn into the path. It leads to a network of other paths with irregular dirt surfaces, passing through the gardens and orchards of private residences.

These paths are called *sentes*, similar in conception to the *ruelles* of Montmagny. The longer form of the word, *sentier,* means "hiking route."

I weave through the *sentes,* enjoying the shade, even under a mid-day sun. Nearing the top, the panorama widens, and I can peek through orchards to view the valley below as well as the wooded ridge beyond the valley, the one I'd enjoyed on Day Sixteen when cycling to the Bois des Eboulures. If I'd brought my binoculars, I could probably catch a glimpse of that monster blue-yellow IKEA store.

Above the *sentes,* I turn into a winding country road. For the moment, I hear no cars so I'll have the road to myself. It marks the border with the Montmorency Forest. Not long after, I come across the pretty church whose backyard cemetery is nestled within the forest. This is the perfect picnic spot: a stone bench under a cluster of shade trees facing the side of the church and the cemetery behind it.

Country cemeteries have freshwater faucets so I can finish my water and refill the bottle. I've brought my favorite smoked-salmon-veggie sandwich from my In-and-Out bakery. I've also got an almond chocolate pastry, and from home I've brought cashews.

I try to elongate my stay in this hidden nook of the forest. I study details of the Eglise Notre-Dame de Taverny, built on the initiative of Lord Mathieu II de Montmorency around the year 1240. In contrast to today's oligarchs, Lord Mathieu fought his own battles rather than sending others to do the dangerous work.

I even consider bike-hiking up into the forest, as I'm not far from the pretty Godard Pond. However, the other half of my Taverny circuit awaits me. The city has sprawled north and south but the high forest barrier on the east has created the natural boundary I just visited and now I will see the west side, whose effective boundary is the railroad line.

This is the day's *West Side Story.* I weave in and out of residential streets where the bicycle is a bit too fast a mode of transportation to appreciate the beautiful rustic houses, each with its own style. From time to time, I stop and gawk. For the most part, these homes were built between the 1880s and 1930s. Some of the homes even have turrets, as if the owners had the illusion of building their private castles.

I am reminded of a red brick Victorian mansion in the Kenwood neighborhood on the south side of Chicago, where I once landed a rent-free period in exchange for shoveling coal into the basement oven, gardening, and washing windows. My neighbor was the Honorable

Elijah Muhammad but no matter how often I walked past his mansion, I never bumped into him.

Kenwood's streets were in grid form, but here I wind in and out and begin to lose my sense of direction. Most of the homes are walled in, attractive stone walls with ivy, but I catch glimpses of wild gardens with-in, as well as intricate brickwork on façades.

I've made a point to stop and jot down the phone numbers on "for sale" signs to compare the prices here with those of Paris, but not a single home is up for sale. These residents have good reason to not market their city to Paris speculators.

Now I am back on Route 928, feeling guilty that cycling in Taverny has been free of all stress. It's almost as if I were sitting on a tourist bus and not a bicycle saddle. I wonder if some degree of stress is necessary for exercise to be productive.

It's 18.5 km from my front door to the center of Taverny, which would make this a round trip of 37 km, and I add one more kilometer to cover for the incursion into the *sentes* and the weaving in and out, back and forth, on the west side of town.

Day 23: 38 km. Trip to date: 564 km.

Day 24

Black Hole Gastronomy

Within the confusing web of trails in Bois de Boulogne are two oases I've never visited. I'm off again to Boulogne but with a different mission: find out what secrets lie within the two retreats that hide within the forest. Is it possible to have one refuge within another?

I am hoping to discover some sort of biological or botanical black hole. I know I'm setting myself up for disappointment, but I've got to find out.

Very quickly I discover that yes, each of these two settings within the forest contains a black hole. They are both pretty places, but contrary to what I'd hoped for, less wild than their surroundings. Thoreau would have blamed the English gardeners.

First stop is a pair of islands connected by a footbridge within the Lac Inferieur at the heart of Bois de Boulogne with pleasantly hilly walking paths. To get onto the islands, you take a free water shuttle. These launches operate regularly, serving a restaurant called "Le Chalet des Iles", but taking the launch does not require that you lunch or even munch at Le Chalet.

The second stop is the Pré Catalan, containing walking paths large enough for a bicycle to do a few figure-eights, an outdoor theatre, and Shakespeare Garden within, as well as the elegant restaurant, Le Pré Catalan.

Both restaurants get multiple stars from Michelin and have famous chefs. Sadly, my ample credentials as a Picnic Reviewer do not qualify me to do Restaurant Reviews.

But I have discovered the nature of these two black holes. They are not astronomical but gastronomical. They are certainly not economical, for they will suck you in for moments of divine pleasure followed by financial stress.

Well, I exaggerate. You can probably dine at Le Chalet for less than 100 Euros and at Le Pré Catalan for less than 300, but if you also order wine with which to dine on cuisine so fine, your credit card may flash "decline" with your logarithm becoming suspicious of this atypical expense.

If such is the case, you may never leave the black hole.

I've managed to evacuate from the black holes. To celebrate, I orbit the entire perimeter of Bois de Boulogne, gaining 26 km for the day by the time I am back to my cosmic campsite.

Day 24: 26 km. Trip to date: 590 km.

Day 25

What Use Is a House without a Healthy Planet to Put It On?

Today will be the shortest outing but will have a deep connection with Thoreau. The group I belong to, Attac92, has organized a walking-bicycling event to defend our green areas against real estate speculation. We are combining the Thoreau of *Walking* and *Life Without Principle* with the Thoreau of *Civil Disobedience*.

A group of us are taking a bike-hike through our city of Clichy in order to celebrate the protests of our neighbors. We're going to document with a photo essay their struggle to stop building speculators from replacing green areas with a parking lot and apartment buildings.

Our first stop is a boulevard called "the Alleys", lined with a rambla-type walking mall with shade trees and flowers down the middle and on both sides. There are benches set in little nooks and crannies amid bushes and flowers. Like the Ramblas of Barcelona, this boulevard has one lane for cars on each side and is lined with well-preserved historic buildings. Unlike the Ramblas, this is not a tourist site and commerce is only sparsely integrated into the scene.

The city wants to build an underground parking lot here, which would uproot many of the trees. From the apartment buildings along the way hang banners: "Save the Trees," "Stop the Assault on Nature," "Stop the Cementing of The Alleys." Our neighbors have won a court victory which puts a temporary stay on any excavating, but they tell us they fear a new round of legal struggles.The next stop is an apartment complex covering an entire block between two parallel streets, with green yards, shade trees, and play spaces for children on each side. These green areas set the building in from the streets. Builders have supposedly purchased the green areas from the owner and want to build seven-floor housing structures. The structures would replace these green areas and cut off the view of the street that the current residents now enjoy.

Once again, banners are hanging from the windows of the apartment complex and from the windows of nearby buildings: "Stop the Construction of a Building in Front of our Windows," "No to Constructing a Building Between Us and the School Across the Street," "Save our Green Space: It's the Lungs of the Whole Neighborhood."

For our final stop, we ride-hike to another corner of the city, where a small-but-cozy park has been eliminated to be replaced by student housing. There are dozens of building sites throughout the city and any one of them could have been used as a student residence.

I can imagine adding Thoreau's sayings to our neighbors' banners, such as: "What is the use of a house if you haven't got a tolerable planet to put it on? (79)

It seems that our neighbors' acts of disobedience would fit with how Thoreau integrates acts against authority with neighborly solidarity: "I am as desirous of being a good neighbor as I am of being a bad subject." (242)

I recall a recent confrontation with a city official. I challenged this unsustainable growth and its assault on green spaces. His response: "We have to increase population density near Paris, in order to prevent pent-up housing pressure from expanding into agricultural territories."

I would like to ask if his solution is a mere Band-Aid for overpopulation. However, that's a can of worms, and I am not knowledgeable on the subject. I didn't have the data available to challenge his use of "growth" to legitimize real estate speculation. I kept my response sweet and green: that "no matter how logically you present the argument, there is no excuse for removing green space."

Following our bike-hike documentation of the assault against nature in Clichy, those of us with bikes cycle into surrounding towns, enjoying the freedom we have on two wheels that Thoreau would have loved.We will publish our findings and distribute them as a tract to show our solidarity with the disobedience of our neighbors.

In the end, I've only done 10 km, but this communion with Thoreau has had a positive effect on my mental health.

Day 25: 10 km. Trip to date: 600 km.

Day 26

Ourcqing

I've cycled the entire Canal Saint-Martin, 4.55 km, and the entire Canal Saint-Denis, 6.6 km, but am I ready for the Canal de l'Ourcq, 96.6 km?

As I've said, when the going gets tough, I look for a peaceful compromise. I set my sights on the Sevran Forest, known as the Parc Forestier National de la Poudrerie. Once I get there, if I continue cycling across the 340-acre forest to its eastern limit, my total ride will be 25 km from my front door. With the round trip, this would become the first 50 km event within the 1,000 km ride.

I decide to pack extra "fuel for fifty." My picnic lunch consists of two bean-rice tacos (I smash the beans and cook whole grain rice). I've got large corn tortillas. Into the taco, I add my own special hot sauce that includes green chilis, diced tomatoes, and fresh aromatic cilantro. It will also include avocado, which I take separately, to be cut open at the picnic bench. With avocados, it's always a gamble. Sometimes you open what appears to be a good avocado, and it's turned dark brown on the inside.

I wrap the tacos in aluminum foil. For dessert, I have a square of 70% chocolate. I've got an orange which I will eat with cashews for a rest stop on the way home.

I'm not a vegan, but vegan fuel seems right for this trip.

I pass a Holiday Inn on the way out of Clichy, and I fear that today's ride will be as exciting as the hotel chain's old adage: "The best surprise is no surprise." What if everything goes so smoothly that I will have nothing to write? *He got on his bike, rode 25 flat kilometers, had a picnic, and then rode back.* As if Thoreau's *Walking* had occurred on a treadmill.

To get to the canal, I must ride the Paris outer boulevard bike lane. The Holiday Inn motto turns ominous. Not a single delivery truck has blocked the bike path. No residents from the drinkers-of-cheap-wine community around La Chapelle have wobbled into my path. I have not even gotten sideswiped by a shooting scooter.

At an intersection, people in a beleaguered tour bus look down on me, and I read the lips of one of the imprisoned passengers, "If I had known bicycling was so easy, I wouldn't have gotten stuck in this damn bus."

Even crossing the boulevard to enter the canal path at Parc de la Villette has been unchallenged but for a few cobblestones. The canal path begins so easily that I fear having to place an asterisk next to my first 50 km day.

With the lazy waters at my side, I'm soothed into forgetting the major problems around me. I should be concerned that all my cycling days have been free from significant rain. It is not normal for the spring season to mimic a pop song. By unconscious association I begin humming "A Beautiful Morning" by the Rascals, released in 1968, depicting a spring morning with no rain and oblivious to the rage against the Vietnam War.

A summer drought has become predictable. Some of the ponds where the herons need to go fishing will dry up. In a worst-case scenario, there will be no more water for the Canal de l'Ourcq and a dead body will be exposed, leading to the re-opening of an unsolved homicide.

These thoughts quickly vanish. The song promotes the need to be optimistic and active. I swerve away from the impending drought and seize my temporary right to be carefree.

I have been told that some degree of anxiety is good, but I fear that my only stressful moment will be cutting open the avocado, to see whether it is soft and green on the inside or blackened and worthless.

The Canal de l'Ourcq is diverse in its context. First, there is Parc de La Villette, dressed in primary colors, the playground of northeast Paris. What follows is a gentrifying industrial zone with tempting canal-side outdoor cafés. There will be parks, then more industry, train yards, a new housing development, and finally a residential neighborhood of the city of Sevran.

Most plane crashes are caused by human error, and I would say that many bike tours have gone awry from human error. At one point, I find myself behind a barrier of a cement factory, and it looks as if they have purposely constructed this barrier to prevent bikes from getting through.

I realize what has happened. I was rolling along singing a complacent song, *It's a beautiful morning …*, and must have missed the detour sign that pointed to a path along SNCF train yards. Getting the bike through the barrier would require one person on each side.

Fortunately, I will not be the only one who has missed the cutoff. Two young women wheel up to the barrier simultaneously, and we help each other get our bikes under the bars. It takes three people, one on each side of the barrier and a third person to direct the operations.

I had never met these two women before but there has been a momentary bond of solidarity: three trespassers committing the same human error get to save each other from a bent wheel or a broken spoke. I consider contacting the cement factory to obtain a video of the sequence; we were trespassing, and there must have been cameras looking down upon us.

Farther ahead, I pass through an elaborate canal party with a coffee maker on a folding table, lawn chairs, and graffiti painters beginning the day's work. From the looks of things, these are not stealth graffiti artists and have probably been hired by local authorities.

From then on, the route flows without any real climbs, and only a pedestrian-bike overpass to the other side involves any hard pedaling. If given the choice, underpasses are easier than overpasses because they begin on a downhill so that you've gathered momentum for the uphill.

I accept the challenge of getting over the twisting overpass without having to get off the bike: one of the rare challenges of Canal de l'Ourcq. I manage the two bends of the bridge without stopping, but a personal trainer would have criticized my form and had me do it again.

Continuing after the overpass, I get to see some choicely-located homes along the canal. I wonder if they get mosquitos at night, but I do know that the engineers who built the canal for Bonaparte in the early 1800s had to make sure there were no stagnant waters (loved by mosquitos), since the intention was to bring potable water to Paris.

The canal has now narrowed, and its banks have risen above it. For a Pantheist, a look through the long shady waterway nave becomes a religious experience.

I've arrived at the official entrance to the *Forêt*. As a former gunpowder manufacturing site (you still see the train tracks), this forest required lots of loving care in order to be transformed into a safe and ecological park in 1973. As late as 2017, they still needed an elaborate decontamination project.

At various intersections of dirt trails, park officials have put up plaques commemorating the work of the volunteer ecological groups. Among the rescued trees are two giant sequoias, doublette oaks, an inclined poplar, and a field elm, now classified as "remarkable trees."

I arrive at a clearing, where I see the two trespassing acquaintances. They've just arrived and are setting up a picnic. I take advantage to have them take my picture. The woman with the cellphone camera takes several angles, seems quite motivated, and clicks to send the photos to my email address.

Turns out they are from Saint-Ouen, the next city after Clichy, so they've ridden nearly as many kilometers as I have. Like many French folks I know, these two women choose a grassy area under the sun. I decide to cycle on to find a place in the shade, where there should be a rustic café.

I find it and grab an outdoor table with bench for myself. Judging from the intersecting melodies, I am listening to a variety of bird species. The Moment of Truth has arrived. Everything is set up, and the last task before my glorious picnic is to open the avocado with the kitchen knife I've brought along.

A good avocado combines perfectly with tomato and cilantro.

I prepare myself for the worst. Even if it's not edible, I still have a great salsa to accompany my tacos. I cut slowly, and there it is: splendid, luminous, silky green.

The return ride is mellow. Beyond the pure pleasure of pedaling, the main feature is the graffiti party, where it looks as if they will finish by the end of the day. The quality of the paints is remarkable, and even the color grey has a sheen to it.

I'm still troubled that I get to claim 50 km for a stress-free, pre-drought ride. I seek comfort from the Active Towns podcast slogan of John Simmerman: "A culture of activity for all ages and abilities." Tomorrow will be another 50 km. However, with long and demanding climbs, there will be no need for an asterisk. Today's steady state ride will have me prepared.

Day 26: 50 km. Trip to date: 650 km.

Fourth Movement:
Bolivar Blues

Days 27 through 32

Warm-up

When I cycle, theme songs go through my head. No need for earphones. "Bolivar Blues" was one of the few Thelonious Monk songs that I was able to work out on the piano. When cycling around La Paz, Bolivia, where "elevation gain" replaces "distance traveled" as a primary cycling goal, Monk's "Bolivar Blues" filtered actively into my mind as I pedaled (and sometimes got off and walked the bike) up steep hills.

The mind plays association games by making hidden connections independently of conscious thought, and surely the fact that I'd known the Bar Thelonious in Sopocachi, La Paz, and that Bolivia was named after the liberator Bolivar, triggered Monk's "Bolivar Blues" to circulate in my mind when confronting my first prolonged climbs.

In this, the fourth movement of the 1,000 km, I finally feel completely recovered and ready to soar.

Day 27

Double Climb

Twice in the past, I had road-cycled from Enghien at 40 meters / 131 feet to the top of the Montmorency Forest at 162 meters / 531 feet, for an elevation gain of 400 feet.

To get here, I pass through the pretty village of Montlignon, stopping along the way to gawk at the funk: haphazard dirt or cobblestone courtyards with bright green hills in the background, colorful townhouse shutters, gritty and grainy elegance, the look of a *beau village*.

At the top of this climb, with forest on both sides, I had twice looked down into a winding descent that would take me to real French farming country, but then failed to take the tempting plunge. I'd feared, in the wake of the 400-foot ascent, that a second climb back up could break me.

I've thus accumulated two strikes without even taking a swing. The agricultural town below, Moisselles, sits at 85 meters / 278 feet altitude, so the re-climb calculated to be 253 feet, for a combined two-climb total of 653 feet in elevation gain. I'd climbed more on a single outing in Bolivia, and that was at a demanding high altitude where each breath of air took in only 60% of the oxygen I am now breathing in.

I survey the terrain. The final kilometer of this second climb in the forest consists of a partly-protected bike lane, steep enough that looking up at the top is almost as painful as looking into the sun. My tactic is to focus on the pavement, creating the illusion that the climb is not nearly as sharp.

These are my thoughts, my strategies, as I contemplate my last opportunity to take the plunge into the sprawling farmland around Moisselles.

From my *Institut Géographique National* contour map, I've gleaned that Moisselles will be one of those *beaux villages*. This time, I take the plunge. The descent is steep, so I know that my return under the early afternoon sun is going to be laborious. Once the terrain flattens out, with a partly canopied bike lane, I can see into the fields of glowing grain, and with the slight descent, I am experiencing a moment of pure pleasure.

The intellect shares in the pleasure as it is reassuring to know that a major city like Paris has farmland within 25 km of downtown. The density proponents in my town argue that if we don't fill every gap with people, right here, that housing will creep outward into the farmlands. That's their argument.

The equivalent of Moisselles, back in Los Angeles, would be to ride over the Hollywood Freeway and find farmland in the San Fernando Valley. Fat chance.

As a town, Moisselles turns out to be a disappointment, but the farmland context is still invigorating. The little river that crosses through Moisselles, Le Petit Rosne, provides irrigation but has been responsible for three great floods within the past century. The name and the town traces back to Muscilla in the year 832. However, no nobleman has ever lived here, and thus, no one built gothic hunting lodges or narcissistic monuments, so the town has remained anonymous, like some of the outwardly-forlorn towns you see from the windows of the train they call "The City of New Orleans," as it rolls between Kankakee and Champaign-Urbana.

I've packed a copious picnic lunch. At my favorite boulangerie along the way, I've bought the best salmon sandwich with goat cheese and veggies, along with a *choco-amande* pastry, the cousin of the *croissante d'amande*. But I am willing to postpone my picnic if I can discover a local restaurant.

In the end, my packed lunch looks better than what they have in the Moisselles local pizza bar, so before lunching, I must cycle back up 253 feet on an empty stomach to have my picnic at the ponds and enjoy the weird example of medieval architecture at the Chateau de la Chasse (Hunters' Castle).

It's worth repeating the mantra that in bicycle touring, the decision of where to eat, finding the perfect picnic spot, replaces the bigger decisions in life, like when to have children or what retirement fund to invest in. With this inversion of the decision pyramid, the pleasure of the moment replaces the anguish of the long-term struggle.

For this second climb, Moisselles to Chateau de Chasse, the sun is partly in my face, but the forest lurks at my sides so I enjoy a fresh breeze. My Bolivian climbs were essentially above the tree line for all but three species of tree, so I can consider this a luxury climb in comparison. I hum Monk's chirpy "Bolivar Blues."

However, it has not been a simple question of arriving at the twin-pond oasis in the Montmorency Forest at the edge of Chateau de Chasse. The sun is beating down directly on all the benches around the lake, so I must walk the bike into the edge of the forest and find a tree trunk that will allow me a view of the ponds.

I've expected to be all alone, but on this weekday afternoon, groups of schoolchildren are rambling by in loosely-organized lines, with teacher and teaching aide leading and following each group like mama and papa mallard. I become the reception end of one *"bon appetit"* after another. I am the only adult in the park who is not tethered to flocks of lively children.

At dessert time, after two heavenly bites of the almond-chocolate pastry, I make the big decision of the day. As delicious as this pastry is, I will save the rest for my concocted "campground" near the end of the ride. I remind myself that with each "return" trip, I need to camp out before arriving at the apartment, to preserve the illusion of an extended voyage.

In the meantime, my return trip rolls down a separate parallel route through Montlignon, and once again, I stop to gawk, this time in the more elegant part of town, with the hills of the forest on both sides and a few structures that look like castles of the less-rich-and-less-famous sector of the leisure class.

I decide that today's campground will be the Parc des Sevines by the exercise machines, a corner of the park that will be empty on this weekday. Awaiting me is "my" bench for stretching out.

With French folks choosing to sit in the sunlight, my shady bench will be empty. I am convinced that the fern must be prominent in my shade-loving genetic heritage. There is Superman, Spiderman, and me: Fernman.

Behind the exercise machines is a thick cluster of trees where I can sneak in invisibly to take a piss. Yes, most of the "amenities" of a stealth campsite are found in this corner of the park.With Parc des Sevines as my intended destination, I descend from the Chateau de la Chasse like a grey heron. In cycling with such ease, I am reminded that I have already accomplished my day's labor on the way up.

The Enghien lake is sparkling and I almost do my pastry stop at its edge, but I decide to stick to the tough decision I arrived at in front of the Chateau de Chasse. Once in the Parc des Sevines, I enjoy my *choco-amande* bite by bite by bite, and then stretch out and relax as if I'd be staying overnight.

The scene is not as perfect as I would want it. Thoughts of Ukrainian, Yemini, and Palestinian refugees remind me that camping out for them is done out of necessity, not out of choice. I've had the luxury of mapping out the day, time, and hour of my own *parcours*. I have a free green art nouveau pump in this "campsite" to fill up my bottle with potable water. I have shade trees, including the splendid jacaranda, with their violet flowers in full season. This is my reality: an alternate reality for the millions who are forced onto the roads in the wind and rain or under the punishing sun.

The energy I use for my travels is my choice. I feel (a matter of perception) wealthier than Bill Gates, Elon Musk, and Jeff Bezos combined, and with only a minute fraction of their carbon footprint. I am tackling a joyous challenge, 1,000 km by bike, significantly more respectful to the health of planet Earth than Jeff Bezos's four minutes in space. And yet, I have been pampered by the luxury that allows me to engage in such a challenge at my own choosing.

Day 27: 50 km. Trip to date: 700 km.

Day 28

Hedonism on Two Wheels

On the last climb from Moisselles to the Chateau de Chasse, I'd felt the beginnings of an off-season heat wave, and today the temperature has risen above my comfort level, nearly 30 degrees Celsius or 85 degrees Fahrenheit. After two consecutive 50 km days, I decide to indulge in the pursuit of maximum pleasure. I map out a route that will keep me, for the most part, under the cover of a splendid canopy, the typical French platane trees, oak trees, beech, pine, and even a redwood tree for picnicking. I have designed my own greenway.

I begin on the bike lanes through Levallois along the Seine and continue over a leafy avenue through Neuilly that must have been designed by royal landscape architects.

I stop at a convenience store to pick up two sandwiches, both marked A in the Nutri-Score rankings, a bag of cashews, and some dried fruit for dessert (a no-no for my vegan friends since the sugar concentration in dried fruit is thought to be excessive).

My route crisscrosses the Bois de Boulogne on paths I have not before taken. The big decision of the day is whether to picnic at the Parc de la Bagatelle or beneath a redwood by a lake in the forest. I choose La Bagatelle and reserve the redwood for another day with a different route.

Though I will accumulate a total of 24 km, today's outing is more like a rest day. My next two days are programmed for longer distances and challenging climbs.

Back in my first week of cycling, this route would have been a chal-lenge. Today it is embarrassingly pleasurable, crossing the border into hedonism. During my picnic, I am passed by a runner who is huffing and puffing and sweating all over. I wonder whether his type of exercise and mine have any similarity or if we are on opposite poles of the physical activity spectrum.

As hedonist for a day, I raise my water bottle to toast the ascetic who is passing me. Tomorrow, I will strive to honor his kind.

Day 28: 24 km. Trip to date: 724 km.

Day 29

Getting High in Bougival

Today's destination is the gothic church that towers above Bougival, set within the hilly woods.

My previous trip to Bougival (Day Twenty-One) ended at the part of the town that touches the river. An expressionist rainstorm was brewing over the hills, and I had to abort half my stay in the town, namely the church on the hill.

The glorious river trail ends abruptly four long blocks before the center of town. For this stretch of earth-scape, I need to get on the main road. However, something happens here that did not happen on the road through Montlignon or the road to Taverny. On those trips, when there was no shoulder on the road, car drivers behind me had to lower their speed and raise their level or patience, which they did.

Here in Bougival, the drivers behind me have no patience and crank up their engines to a frightening pitch. The drivers may not want to kill me, but their engines do.

Normally I can resist intimidation and roll along humming Monk. But in this case, I feel a life-and-death situation and prudently pull the bike up on the curb of a sidewalk too narrow to ride on.

I wonder if this is a local cultural difference. Both Montlignon and Taverny are in the Department of Val d'Oise. Bougival is in the Department of Yvelines. French departments may differ in their traffic rules and the social engineering that accompanies them (Yvelines is the fifth of France's 95 mainland departments that I've ridden in during this 1,000 km bike saunter).

It could also be the fact that between the Seine and the town, the hills bend straight up with no space for an alternate parallel road.

I make it to the corner of the street that climbs to the church: Eglise Notre-Dame de l'Assomption. The climb is lined by local commerce with colorful awnings and with residential apartments above the shops, in typical French village style.

The church is set into a ledge with woods at its side and a garden in front. I'd love to engage with the locals and ask for a photo, but I see only a woman who is watering the garden, one of the faithful, and she has no phone with her.

I find another woman who approaches me with a bright smile. It's her job to welcome people into the weekday non-prime time mass. She's probably disappointed that I'm not here to attend, but as a church volunteer, she's thrilled to take pictures in which I am but a small mosaic scrap in the larger Byzantine design, which will glorify her beautiful church.

She shows me the pictures and asks which one to send, I pick out one that looks professional and whose great angle highlights the gothic wonders, and she clicks on the send button. (I later find out that the picture never arrived at my email address for some reason.)

I have a chance to duck in and see the interior before mass, with its high vaulted ceiling, Notre Dame style, and I have fulfilled the vows of the day's pilgrimage. I would have liked to say hello to Father Bonnet, but he is about to begin a service for the funeral of Mademoiselle Odette Simon. I do not know who this woman is or if she died as a child or an adult.

At the church garden, a woman approaches me, asking if this is the church where they will have a funeral service. She's obviously not from Bougival. She seems quite distraught. I've read the church pamphlet and know this is indeed the site of the funeral service, and I find myself in the uncomfortable situation of guiding someone to a place I know nothing about.

I think about the dead person. As "mademoiselle", she was never married. Maybe she chose it that way. Perhaps she died as a child. As one who is cycling 1,000 km to deny my own inevitable death, I am shaken by the death of someone I have never known.

My return to the river means cycling downhill, legally, against the the traffic on a one-way street with no curbs. On my way down, the only barrier is an Italian restaurant whose lunch tables spill out onto the street. I take care not to sideswipe any tables, to not send spaghetti plates flying down the hill.

I find a convenience store to purchase the oranges and bananas I need for my temporary residence on Earth and am on my way, or so I think. But once more, I must contend with the inhumane riverside road until I make it back to the river path. This time I stay on the road, engaging in vehicular cycling. In 2019, the most recent statistic, Bougival only had two injuries due to car crashes and zero deaths. My perception that the cars behind me contain enemy drivers may be erroneous.

Once on to the bike-pedestrian path, I enjoy flowing along with the river for 15 km, taking a higher and hilly parallel path when it materializes. People are swarming in the parklands, enjoying yet another perfect spring day, perhaps oblivious to the probable drought that could follow this rain-free spring.

I feel like shouting out to everyone: "A minute of silence for Mademoiselle Odette Simon," but of course, that would be a useless gesture. My thoughts on this matter are slowly emerging from my brain, which is stuck in first gear.

Once out of the Seine à Vélo, I climb three hills to get back home. I look forward to the feel-good fatigue.

But then I realize that my slow thinking has once more caused me to miss the moment. As a sign of solidarity, perhaps we should attend the funerals of people we do not know. Especially people who may have led "lives of quiet desperation" or people who were never given a chance in the first place.

If I had a brain that pedaled as fast as my feet, I would have decided to attend the funeral on the hill atop Bougival.

Day 29: 42 km. Trip to date: 766 km.

Day 30

Good Climbs and Good Times

My objective for the day is the town Montmorency and its secretive trails, called *sentes*. This will be my third look at peri-urban farming, following Montmagny and Taverny, and all three are in the foothills of the Montmorency Forest.

To get to the actual town of Montmorency, I plan on rolling through Montmagny then climbing to Montmorency. Following the Montmagny city hall, the route I've marked turns out to be one-way with no contra-flow markings, so I take a parallel route which then twists away from where I want to go, winding downward into a hollow, where the pretty town of Groslay is cradled.

I'm happy to have been diverted, since I get to see the grainy stone-work on the Eglise Saint-Martin de Groslay and especially to enjoy the winding streets lined with colorful Ma-and-Pa commerce. I seek a mathematical equation for what I see. Ma and Pa here in French suburbs are still out there selling things, whereas it seems as if Ma and Pa in American suburbs are at Walmart or Home Depot, buying things. I'm not sure how I can balance this equation.

I ask Sprawl-Buster Al Norman. He sends me the math, from his "Slam-Dunking Walmart": "In the first decade after Walmart entered Iowa, 7,326 small businesses—grocery stores, hardware stores, apparel stores—went under. Wal-Mart hit these towns with the force of 100 new businesses opening at once. People were left with nowhere to shop but the Big Box."

My downward detour that has given me this happy retro-landing in Groslay means I will face a longer climb to Montmorency: nearly 300 feet.

It's a seignorial road with 19th century manors and gardens along the climb to Montmorency. At one juncture, I decide to leave one type of beauty in exchange for another, taking a detour through orchards at the foot of the forest with narrow paths (*sentes*) crisscrossing through. Some of these paths are wide enough for a bike and others narrow into walking corridors, separating private orchards and farmland.

Throughout France, there's an agreement between state or city and local inhabitants that hiking paths can cut through private property. These trails exist because users, through their hiking groups, have stipulated that the landscape will be respected.

I settle on a place for a picnic: under a tree with a bulging base serving as a bench. My view includes apple and pear orchards as well as free-ranging chickens with two superb bourgeois manor houses in the hills behind the orchards.

A young woman passes by on what seems to be her daily jog. I move my stretched legs so she can pass, but then realize that she has a cellphone that can take a picture of this wonderful site.

She seems exuberant about the photo-op and has me stand at two different angles to make sure that at least one of them comes out. It's nice to exchange smiles with the only other member of my species I will see on this path.

From my picnic nest, I look through the wire fence at a few hens who are exploring aimlessly, as I am. One of the earliest Disney cartoons portrayed egg-laying hens on strike against the farmer. The free-roaming hens I am watching have it pretty good. In our local food markets, I have observed that we've passed a tipping point. Consumers in our working-class neighborhood now reject industrially produced eggs and overwhelmingly are willing to pay a slightly higher price for the eggs produced by free-roaming hens. This is a small sign that it will be possible to reach a critical mass of steady state way-of-lifers.

I let my mind wander like the hens. Will a Tour de France bicycle racer ever enjoy a chance to get off the bike and walk it through a sanctuary like this one at the foot of Montmorency?

These crisscrossing paths take me up to a high spot and then reach a street lined with large stone-worked homes and profuse gardens as I enter the town of Montmorency. I must have done lots of climbing because it's mainly downhill on the way back, and I hardly have to pedal. Ivan Illich was right. The bicycle is the most energy-efficient mode of travel. I entertain a wild dream that the stories I tell might inspire regions around the world to improve infrastructure for active living that will be fit for all ages and abilities.

This author on a bike confronts promotional limitations. But put Thoreau on the bike, and we have a better chance.

Day 30: 34 km. Trip to date: 800 km.

Day 31

Searching for Escape Route #6

Today I have a chance to relive a science fiction story by Clifford Simac about a young couple living in a utopia where all of life's needs were provided. After much deliberation, the couple decided to explore outside their oasis and discover what lay beyond the utopia. The providers of plenty had told the citizens that the only law to be followed was to not stray beyond the boundaries of the utopia.

This couple's curiosity was too strong. They took the risk. They departed from their daily gardens and began walking. But no matter how far or for how long they walked, they kept ending up in the same place of departure.

I already have my five utopian bike escape routes. I have no need for more, except perhaps to enhance the sensation of the road trip, to find out what lies beyond. After all, the bicycle should be a vehicle for exploration.

I am attracted by a little known peri-urban time warp area that would be best reached if I could find the northeast passage. The only problem is that my intended route would need to pass through a no-man's land, a disjointed and chaotic corner of Saint-Denis, one of the poorest cities in France and now subject to a massive gentrification-speculation project called *Le Grand Paris*.

Before my departure, I plot a potential course. I choose Route D410, which sports an old bike path through the city of Saint-Ouen.

The bikelane is currently under repair, but at least it is symbolically comforting.

The problem begins at the border between Saint-Ouen and Saint-Denis. With freeways passing overhead and construction sites on all sides, it is a scene from *Robocop*. I am forced by "Detour" signs into a right turn, and then the road hits endings at construction sites, with more "Detour" signs, or simply arrows in only one possible direction. I try to straighten out my route, keeping right, but the curvature of the road now bends me left. Here and there, there is an occasional stray café, slated for demolition.

You may ask if I've been stupid to not use GPS. I can tell you that on two occasions with my tech friend Daniel driving, his GPS got us lost and my visceral sense of direction got us back on the right road. In this ever-changing landscape, yesterday's routes are subject to today's detours, whose arrows may change direction tomorrow.

I come to a juncture at which the left turn is a clearly demarcated road while the right turn that I probably need would take me into an orange forest of tall construction cranes. I take the left, intending to take the next available right-turn option.

To my surprise, I end up at Ile-Saint-Denis, at a direct route back home. I wish Clifford Simac could tell my story.

The search for the escape route is temporarily aborted, since I am not willing to backpedal into the chaotic maze of detours I've just survived.

I resolve not to give up, to try again with better preparation. I now know what to avoid. My awareness of geography and sense of direction tells me that some viable northeast escape route must exist. I vow to find it. In the meantime, I put my bike in the *cave* (the basement) and walk up 60 steps to my little utopia.

Day 31: 18 km. Trip to date: 818 km.

Day 32

Coffee Break in Paris

On this planned day off, I've found an excuse for getting on the bike: a coffee break on a Parisian balcony. I'm riding into Paris to meet with friends who were volunteers in the 2016 and 2020 Bernie Sanders "global primary" campaigns.

I am able to do today's ride, and hopefully the entire projected 1,000 km, thanks to my hernia operation and the help of preventive measures that the French mainly single-payer health care system affords us.

It's pleasing to ride the bike-friendly Boulevard Rochechouart, below Montmartre. Its complete street design includes outer perimeter sidewalks, single-lane street space for cars and buses, interior bike lanes separated from the motor vehicles, a pedestrian stroll zone in the treelined center, and the Metro underneath. I once stopped here to tally the mode share between bikes and cars. The bike-to-car ratio was 44:56 during that weekday slice of time.

Paris will never come near Amsterdam or Copenhagen in bicycle mode share because the greater density of Paris and its efficient metro system give residents viable transportation options. In fact, nearly half of all journeys within Paris are on foot, which helps explain why only 5% of trips are by bicycle.

I feel pizzazz in my legs and an ease in my breathing as I whiz down the crowded Magenta Boulevard, faster than the surrounding car traffic but with hands on the brakes in anticipation of the inevitable stray pedestrian.

We sit on the balcony near Republique, sipping freshly-brewed coffee and asking ourselves how it was possible that Bernie won both global primaries by wide margins. In Paris alone, he got 70% of the vote in 2016 and well over 60% in 2020.

We would like to believe that our canvassing made the difference, but he did equally well in the other European countries that were part of the global primary's 17 convention delegates.

There's one common denominator. All these countries have some form of single-payer universal healthcare. You cannot bamboozle Americans abroad with a "how will you pay for it?" response to Medicare for All. Bernie won here mainly on that issue.

Most of the 22 years I've lived in France have been under cost-conscious conservative governments which largely support the healthcare system. No one in Europe views universal healthcare as "socialist." Even the mother of all privatizers, Margaret Thatcher, did not break up the British public healthcare system.

In my former freelance language consulting, I'd have coffee with many French business managers. They felt that any denationalizing of the healthcare system (it is a blend of public and private) would make it much more costly for them to run a business for it would force them to deal with employee health coverage.

My family doctor, who prescribed the laboratory test to objectify the extent of my hernia, has a private practice. Amazingly, he has no need for a medical secretary because the single payer allows for all payments to be standardized with one swipe of a *Carte Vitale*.

As we sip our freshly brewed coffee, we all agree that universal healthcare is close to a steady state sector of the French economy since it is not tied to a growth industry. The incentives are to avoid medical intervention whenever possible, with investment in prevention and lifestyle strategies that do not involve money exchanges.

None of us seated on this balcony have ever heard of anyone in France engaging in a GoFundMe campaign to raise money for healthcare costs, something that has become a regular narrative in American local news stories.

On my way back home, I look around at people in the streets, bicycle riders crisscrossing every which way. I reflect on how the supermarkets have no parking lots because people get there on foot. I pass by a string of art nouveau Metro entrances and sometimes cycle in wide lanes that we share with buses.From what I see around me, I understand that the positive comparative statistics for the French healthcare system may be more complex than simple medical care. With walkable cities where most inhabitants use public transportation, healthy activity is engrained in daily life. France's longer healthy life expectancy may have more to do with people shopping on foot, wheeling supermarket caddies, working 300 fewer hours per year than Americans, and yes, using bikes instead of cars for their commutes.

As I cycle back through Paris, I see the cafés brimming with laidback people who may already be living a joyously frugal life. Only one in three Paris households own a car. Apartments are small by American standards. Perhaps it is by working less and consuming less that so many Parisians can "afford" the hours with friends at their local hangout: their neighborhood living room.

Day 32: 22 km. Trip to date: 840 km.

Fifth Movement:
Breakthroughs

Days 33 through 39

Warm-up

I am nearing the end of the 1,000 km, seriously debating with myself about ending at 999. I do not want to cross a finish line. There is too much that I have missed. Extending distance is good, but I also need to broaden my dimensions.

Why have I missed so much? I have the impression that when cycling through the most beautiful places, I have been merely flirting with all the beauty, going too fast. I am searching for the elusive intimacy with all nature, including human nature.

I'm still looking to "gain" kilometers, yet a deeper purpose tells me to slow down. This is a "discovery" that greeting-card makers had been repeating. I decide that some clichés, some platitudes, are not throwaways, that they contain truths that so-called deeper thought is too arrogant to accept. I review my original rule:

Each outing must have a new destination, a place worthy of a stopover on a road trip, to help create the illusion of a long trip.

But what about the magnificent habitats, and their sense of place, that I have cycled *through,* without smelling the jasmines; without gliding the palm of my hand over the bark of redwoods or beech trees; without taking out binoculars and looking at birds wading, fishing, pooping, swooping; without deepening human contacts?

I decide that within my rule, there should be enough suppleness that I can return to a place at a deeper level, a level of authentic newness. Maybe not new destinations but deeper destinations, more or less what good jazz musicians do when performing enriching variations on a theme.

I decide to make some returns to apparently "same destinations" but with entirely new paths, with greater intimacy as the goal. This new approach considers three new focuses:

Bike walking. I had whizzed by seductive trails that were unbikable. I would now get off the bike and walk it through those trails (as I had done through the *sentes* in Montmorency).

Bird watching. I would take my binoculars and settle into a place, waiting for birds to put on a show.

Chance acquaintances. How can solidarity be expressed with people I will probably never meet again?

These approaches involve spending more time but gaining fewer kilometers: a way of expanding and intensifying this 1,000 km ride.

Day 33

The Search Continues for Escape Route #6

The search for escape route #6 continues ominously, even before I take my bike out of the basement storage room. Once I get down there, I realize that I do not have the needed wrench to tighten the bike saddle, which has been slipping of late, even when I use the tightening latch.

I do not want to go back upstairs to look for the missing large wrench. Instead, I tighten the brakes on our other bike with a small Allen wrench I have in my backpack. The tightening works perfectly for the left brake, while the right break will only partly tighten.

At this moment, in the dark basement, I come to the realization that I do not measure up to Thoreau in the realm of self-reliance. Without a doubt, he would have mastered bicycle mechanics, a skill I am lacking. I do occasional bike repairs at a local association called Solicycle that makes workspace and tools available and has on-premises help if advice is needed. I remain dependent on this help. I repeat a message to myself: I will continue to chase the art of bicycle mechanics in the name of Thoreau's philosophy, but my bikes do not break down frequently enough for me to accumulate the experience. I fix something, a year flies by, and then forget how I fixed it.

The brakes are now functional, so I depart from what we call *le cave* and am on my way. This time, I rectify the original sin from the initial search for the sixth escape route. Once past the Saint-Ouen city hall, instead of continuing over the hellish Route D410, I make a right turn on Rue du Landy.

Precisely at this corner, I see a sign announcing that a fully protected bike lane will soon be constructed along Rue du Landy. On my map, this apparently non-descript street will take me safely through the dense suburbs leading to canal towpaths and other easily-bikeable routes extending to parks and greener horizons to the east.

In medieval antiquity, Rue du Landy was known as Lendit. As with other axis streets in the Paris region, Rue du Landy acquired its functionality in antiquity. A map dating back to 1570 shows Rue du Laendi as the warfront in the battle of 1567. A later map from around 1700 calls it *Le Chemin de Landy,* with *chemin* at the time referring to thoroughfares for long distance coach travel.

Rue du Landy has barely survived the brutality of 1970s suburbanization and is now on its way to becoming revitalized. Using an old and faded bike lane that is no longer functional, I consider myself a pioneer, preparing the terrain for the new bike path and the conviviality that will come with it.

I stop at a boulangerie looking for a sandwich. It's Sunday, a day off for local workers, and sandwiches have not been prepared. I cross the Canal Saint-Denis, and then, using side streets through Aubervilliers, I make it to my destination: the sprawling Parc Departemental George Valbon, popularly known as Parc de la Corneuve. Like Gennevilliers, the La Corneuve municipality is still governed by the French Communist Party.

La Corneuve has produced dozens of French artists, rappers, and leading sports personalities. For many years, the Parc de la Corneuve hosted the legenday *Fête de l'Humanité,* the weekend in September when the French Communist Party joins the mainstream for three days, with a half million attending, before it fades into the background for the rest of the year.

I arrive in Parc de la Corneuve side-by-side with a grandfather who is taking his 9-year-old granddaughter on a bike ride. Given the traffic on the streets leading to the park entrance, my nerves would have been tested to the extreme if I'd have been responsible for a granddaughter on a bike. But he lets her trail behind us with stoic serenity.

He hears my accent, speaks a few words in English, and asks about life in New York. This park offers the bike rider a choice of wooded trails, some of them hilly, or a lakefront ride, out in the open with a view of the Island of the Grey Herons.

The temperature has reached the high '80s, beyond my comfort level, so I keep within the woods for most of the time, parting from Grandpa as he guides his granddaughter into the sun. The crucial rains are nowhere in the advance forecasts. I've not brought a lunch and must settle for some junk food at the snack stand, served up by employees dressed as chefs.

My mission is accomplished. I've identified a legitimate escape route, one with deep history that is slated to be revitalized.

On my return, I explore other routes, finding ways to get lost. My errant riding should be pardoned for with each intersectional choice of a route through either a tree canopy or a sun-bathed commercial zone, I veer automatically away from the sun, the opposite of what my plant friends would do.

I am lost in grey industrial zones, whose long walls stop me from going in the needed direction. I trust that a longer shady route will be more refreshing than a shorter sun-bathed route.

As Thoreau would have done, I wonder about the people who work in these industries, whether they have the free time to enjoy a bike ride in the country. "It would be glorious to see mankind at leisure for once. It is nothing but work, work, work" (*Life Without Principle*, 1).

The worship of leisure that I have observed in Parc de la Corneuve contradicts the scene in the vast industrial zones, where there is no aesthetic relief.

If I had a chance to debate Thoreau on the subject, as he was a willing listener, I would note that people in La Corneuve and the rest of France work 300 hours less per year than people in Concord, Massachusetts and the rest of the United States.

He would have observed increasing numbers of people on bicycles, including grandfathers with their granddaughters, but alas, cycling through wounded regions whose biodiversity is depleted.

I finally recognized a familiar route and make it back to my impermanent hearthside, reflecting on whether the parks and forests I am discovering every day are mere Band-Aids covering up the demise of our habitat, or whether they represent a longshot chance to restore our fundamental partnership with the grey herons.

Day 33: 30 km. Trip to date: 870 km.

Day 34

Forest of Discord

A new method of travel is planned for today. I'll visit the opposite side of the immense Montmorency Forest. Once I cycle into the forest, I intend to detour from the paved Route des Parquets canopy by hiking the bike up some rough hill trails that I've never before entered.

I have trouble getting out of bed. I consider taking the day off. My fresh-brewed espresso tastes great but does not contain the answer to my lethargy. My vegan friends would blame the sugar in the choco-almond pastries.

The only remedy is to get on the bike and ride through the inertia. I am facing a 150-meter elevation gain, nearly 500 feet. It's no consolation that it will be mostly downhill on the return.

How is it, I ask, that in La Paz, Bolivia at 12,000 feet above sea level, I have done climbs of 300 meters, nearly 1,000 feet, but today, half of that seems like too much. Am I nearing the end of my road?

As I enter Montlignon, the gradient increases, sucking my attention away from the pretty town nestled in green hills. I arrive at a deserted traffic circle where I must twist left and do the type of climb that would count as the "Intensity Interval" in high intensity interval training (HIIT).

I've managed this hill in the past, but today, two-thirds up, I'm forced to get off the bike and push for twenty-some yards. Then, I'm back in the saddle. Usually at the top, I feel as if I've "made it!" but in today's state of sluggishness, I feel heaviness in my legs and my breathing. Is it me, or is there an eerie malaise lurking within the forest?

Even as Route des Parquets flattens out, it keeps gaining altitude. I still have 68 m or 220 ft to climb to get to the Godard Pond.

The bike-hike I've planned is a way to climb higher but with less stress. With each rutty hiking trail side trip along the way, I get off and push the bike up to the top of the center ridge of the forest, then back down in a forward direction.

These triangular routes add distance and elevation gain but muffle the acuteness of the climbing. (It is here, in Octobers, where one can come with baskets and pick free chestnuts: 70% of the trees in this wounded forest are chestnut trees. The farther from the road, the bigger the chestnuts you'll find. You will be in competition with seasoned chestnut gatherers.)

This place should be an ecological delight, but Thoreau would be deeply concerned about the wood shearing that I can see on both sides as I push the bike. Entire sections have been either cut down or thinned out. Thoreau would say that this forest is living "in quiet desperation."

I am reminded of my superb trip through Taverny, Day 35, because I see the name of the Taverny mayor, Florence Portelli, as the organizer and top signer of a petition addressed to the Ministers of Agriculture and Environment, protesting the excess tree cutting in the Montmorency Forest.

Portelli is an active member of the traditional right-leaning party of former presidents Jacques Chirac and Nicolas Sarkozy. Her petition has support of people from the entire political spectrum. The cutting down of trees within Montmorency appears excessive for what is needed to combat the chestnut ink disease that has been attacking the forest. Many of the citizens of Montlignon (where I just came from) agree with the Taverny mayor and have signed on.

The petition demands that there be an independent audit of the forest management, which is under the responsibility of the ONF (National Office of Forestry). Until this audit is completed, the petition calls for a moratorium on tree-cutting.

In response to the petition, the National Forestry Office tells its side of the story: since 2018, the Montmorency Forest has been under attack from the microscopic pathogen called ink disease, which destroys the root system of the chestnut trees and will cause a "generalized death" of these trees. The extent of this infestation has been accelerated by global warming, the ONF writes, in particular the warmer winters followed by the more humid springs.

We need to add a new stanza to Nat King Cole's "Chestnuts Roasting on an Open Fire."

The cut trees are being replaced mainly by sessile oaks, which are more resistant to the higher temperatures. I learn that the cut trees are being sold as biofuels to biomass heating plants that depend on wood cuttings. The ONF responds that it only collects between six to eight thousand Euros per cut hectare, a paltry amount, inadequate to call this a profitable operation.

I came here for peace and solitude, not to be in the middle of a political conflict. I notice bird populations seem to have departed from this forest, and the more passionate choral chirping in smaller parks supports my hypothesis. Thoreau would understand: "How can you expect the birds to sing," he wrote, "when their groves are cut down?" (132).

I perceive a result of this productive forest: the disappearance of biodiversity. Montlignon inhabitants have seen fleeing deer and wild boar on their streets.

I feel a profound loneliness as I do the triangular hikes in and out of the deep woods. At first, I assume the loneliness has to do with the absence of Martha, my wife and hiking partner. But another absence perturbs me. I have not seen a single small mammal. Where are my mammal cousins? I try the Thoreau method: "You only need to sit still long enough in some attractive spot in the woods that all its inhabitants may exhibit themselves to you by turns" (155).

This technique fails. One forestry expert has told me that this absence of small mammal wildlife is partly due to over-management of the forests.

I recall the words of Brian Czech in his *Steady State Herald* article "True Conservation: a 21st Century Vision for the Next Director of the Fish & Wildlife Service."

Czech explains that climate change is only the fourth crisis of the past 150 years, following overhunting, habitat loss, pollution, and global heating. We need experts in wild biology conservation, Czech explains, and I recall that Thoreau was already asking for conservation of the wild and often classified the small mammals he saw on his hiking paths. I see none of those mammals, not even a chipmunk, not even the jackrabbits I saw on Ile Saint-Denis in this shell of a once-magnificent forest.

I observe evidence of a few sick trees here and there, but I have no historical reference to compare the same sites with the pre-2018 scene. The petition seems fair enough in simply calling for an official audit and moratorium but does not highlight this loss of biodiversity.

The larger context of this local conflict between the towns surrounding Montmorency and the Office of Forestry is climate change, according to forestry department scientists.

Today, the voluminous records that Thoreau kept of bloom times and weather conditions are being used by climate scientists to track the effects of global warming in the New England states. Among the hikers I see roaming around are probably local Thoreaus, keeping track of this wounded forest.

After several triangular loops up and down the trails, I find myself at my picnic spot at the Godard Pond, 40 meters above the city of Taverny. The grief I have felt at having passed through an entirely bald section of forest is tempered only by the fact that the 25,000 petition signers will eventually settle with the French Office of Forestry on the best way to manage this infestation.

The local mayors around the Montmorency Forest lament the wood cutting, but none of their petitions refer to the fundamental cause of this disaster: infinite growth on a finite planet. This is explained by Brian Czech as he thoroughly refutes the thesis that "there's no conflict between growing the economy and protecting the environment".

Nor do they question the use of biomass, which depends on tree cuttings, as an alternative energy. Even more perverse: European countries are importing wood cuttings from around the world for biomass energy.

I sit on a bench, take a deep breath through my nostrils, let out the air slowly, and ask how it is possible that activists have not come up with a simple solution: consume less. Consume much less and be much happier. Healthier, as well.

My return trip is mainly downhill. I breeze through the forest on the Route des Parquets, feeling privileged and spoiled for gaining pleasure from this flawed and conflicted setting, a forest that will most likely be saved, while forests in many other parts of the world will not be so fortunate.

My lethargy has disappeared. I'd like to congratulate myself for having ridden through the weariness, but objective analysis tells me to get real. My renewed sense of power largely results from the ever-present but mysterious force of gravity. Human intervention has not yet damaged the force of gravity.

Day 34: 40 km. Trip to date: 910 km.

Day 35

Looking for Alain "*Le Poète*"

Had some reckoning to do about my ride two days ago. The hills should have been relatively easy. A few days earlier, it would have been smooth sailing, but I had to get off and push the bike for a few meters just to collect myself.

Simply an off day, or am I reaching the limits of incrementalism?

Today should have happened yesterday but for a knock on the door from the concierge. A water crisis in the building is coming from our apartment. She checked the water pipes inside a trap door behind the toilet. Turns out that my kitchen sink is done for. It could have been my back that went out, or my knee, but it's the kitchen sink.

I had to wait for the plumber. By the time he arrived, it was too late to get out on the road. Kitchen sink pipes, no chance of survival. So far, my internal human plumbing has survived. The plumber will send an estimate later this week. When I heard the e-word, I knew it was no small fix.

The water boiler is also threatening to expire despite having it for only five years. More programmed obsolescence. Everything around me is crumbling except my own body. It, too, is programmed to deteriorate and then to reach a final sputter. But today, it's intact. Forget about tomorrow, it's all about today.

For the time being, life is simplified. One faucet in the bathroom pinch-hitting for the kitchen faucet. Dishes and face washing in the same place. Looking much more like a real campsite. Getting nearer to Thoreau's cabin.

Today, I decide to do three different things. I will test myself on the moderate hills in Chanteraines for confidence building; I will finally stop to do some bird watching; and I will take a pre-COVID route to search for acquaintances I've missed during the pandemic, especially Alain, the 90-year-old-plus who does slow (extremely slow) hiking with a cane and is a volunteer storyteller for schoolchildren on field trips.

I'm quickly down in the *cave* ready to beat the heat, and again, I've forgotten to look for the damn wrench. The latch on my saddle will loosen with bumps in the road, but I don't want to waste time going back up the 60 steps to the apartment to look for the wrench, losing precious minutes as the temperature rises.

Once again, I get out the Allen wrench and tighten the brakes on the older bike, but this time I feel that bike will still be unsafe.

All I need is the wrench for my main bike, to tighten the bolt around the seat pole, but it could take an hour to find it. The heat wave will weigh too heavy in the afternoon. I decide on a temporary solution: I'll ride the good bike like a trotting horse, standing up in the saddle for the bumps.

I'm on my way, and I choose the road instead of the greenway for the smooth surface. Between the apartment and Chanteraines, I need to stop only once to tighten the saddle.

Once into the park, I continue to choose pavement over dirt path. My stop at the birdwatching station proves to be unsuccessful, as I can spot only one black cormorant and a few laughing gulls (*mouettes rieuses*), the ones with the black head on a white body, aside from the usual suspects like the Canadian geese.

Canadian geese were introduced into European and Asian countries, and today they seem to have taken imperialist control over parklands on three continents. Considered by some to be aggressive pests, I learned to admire one Canadian goose when I saw her take a swipe at a muskrat, another introduced species, and send that invader waddling away.

I come away from the moment thinking that if bicycle commuters massively occupied the roads the way Canadian geese occupy the parklands, a critical mass would materialize, and softer and sweeter transportation would bring clean air and happiness.

I will return to this birdwatching stand later to continue my search for less imperial fowl after I've completed the rest of my circuit.

I stop at the only food concession within the sprawling park, La Rainette, where I treat myself to a pondside Lavazza espresso. The plan is to sip while I use my binocs to check out a corner of still water where long-legged wading birds stop to repeat their wordless catch-a-fish mantra.

They are not here.

I've timed my stop in order to catch up with the 90-year-old slow hiker, Alain, one of my inspirations. I haven't looked for him since pre-COVID days. He usually stops at La Rainette, sets down his cane, and enjoys his mid-hike lunch. He *really* enjoys it, eating as slowly as he walks, relishing each bite. His image could be therapy for inveterate fast eaters.

I ask the server at La Rainette for the whereabouts of the old hiker with a cane. "Oh, you're talking about '*Alain le poète.*' Haven't seen him in a long time," he says.

I feel like telling this guy, "Hey, he's your best customer, you can show a little concern."

Lots of 5-to-9-year-olds are in the park on field trips. I ask one of the teachers about "the old man who tells stories to your kids."

"That's *Alain l'auteur.* We haven't seen him in a long time."

Alain is not here.

The man would never miss his daily hike. I have dark suspicions, which I compress into a craven euphemism. Perhaps he is "no longer with us."

Once out of the park and riding on one of the dirt towpaths along the Seine, my saddle is no longer holding, even when I stand up for the mildest bumps, even when I push on the pedal instead of the saddle to get on and off the bike.

I try to remain positive. I think back to the video "How to ride out of the saddle," in which Tom Danielson explains that standing helps you become a better cyclist, helps you with climbing, makes it easier on your back, shoulders, and neck, and gives you opportunities to accelerate and decelerate.

I try to drop my body weight into the pedal stroke, but in the end, I do not have the physical gifts to make this a successful measure.

No excuse for my infantile impatience! I could have gone back upstairs and searched for the wrench. Better to ride firmly in the afternoon heat than ride insecurely when the day is still cool. I've always hated impatience, especially when it is my own.

I contemplate foregoing my second stop at the birdwatching stand and going directly home, over smooth pavement with no saddle-shaking bumps, and then finally doing what I should have done a long time ago: find the wrench.

At that moment, I come upon two bike travelers, looking much like husband and wife. They have panniers on their bikes, meaning that they are on a long trip, so the odds are that they will have a wrench. Random good fortune seems to have appeared at this unlikely time and place.

I ask for help. The man ignores my shout and keeps riding ahead on the dirt path. So much for the famous solidarity of bike travelers.

But the woman has stopped.

"Sorry," she says, in good old American English, "I don't speak French. He kept on cycling because he's deaf and couldn't hear you. Yes, we do have a wrench. When he sees I'm not by his side, he'll pedal back here."

She tells me they are from Eugene, Oregon. When the man returns, I point to the saddle, point to the tightening latch that is not holding, point to the bolt that needs tightening. He gets out the wrench, and it's fixed in 3 seconds.

She asks me to ride a few yards just to vouch that it's secure. I ride in a little circle, a mini victory lap. At this moment, a stable bicycle becomes the essential meaning of life.

I make a mental note to reread *The Improbability Principle* to find out why rare events, million-to-one events, happen every day.

The couple is having the time of their lives, on a voyage of discovery. Their smiles are energizing. They have gone out of the way from any pragmatic route to find this stray path, just when I was passing by. I am inspired by the synchronicity.

Eventually, my repeat hill climb is done in 3rd gear instead of 2nd. This measurable improvement has much to do with both human psychology and the steady saddle. Perhaps the Lavazza espresso as well.

Once back at the birdwatching stand, I luck out. A guy is leaning through the open space in the wood portal with a big zoom lens pointing out at the birds on the rocky edge of the lake. I think, "Maybe Thoreau would have made an exception from his normal disdain for modern conveniences and used a zoom lens." He could have viewed every minute detail at the other side of Walden Pond: the wildflowers, the muskrats, the wading birds.

This friendly man is probably a decade younger than I am. His name is Armand. With a smile as wide as the smiles of the Oregonians, he becomes my instant birdwatching guide. I tell him that the grey heron has been absent. He tells me to bend my neck and point my binoculars to the far left, and sure enough, I spot the old grey heron. I also spot a whitish-grey bird I cannot identify. Armand tells me it's an uncommon cormorant, like an albino.

He promises, with exuberant generosity, to send me photos. (This guy is a serious photographer, the type not apt to give away his artwork. Yet, two days later, his bird pictures arrive as attachments in my email.)

Before leaving Chanteraines, I come upon a chance discovery. Sitting on rows of fence posts are bright red dragonflies. They are also called red-veined darters. I later learn that the males of this species like to be exposed on a perch. Even as I move closer, they do not fly away. Unlike the herons, the red-veined darters are exhibitionists.

My next step is at the weightlifting apparatus in the Parc des Sevines. I have timed my arrival to look for a bicycle friend (we've never exchanged names but always embraced) right here. He does 20 km per day on a prescribed route, ending here.

He has been my ad hoc weight-lifting trainer. Last time I saw him, pre-COVID, he was 82 years old, looking like an Olympian, wiry solid, steely flat stomach, and thanking me profusely (why me?) for the American troops in France and the defeat of the Nazis. Mainly, he's taught me the most efficient way to use the two lifting exercise apparatus.

He's told me stories about the heroic American troops at Hôpital Beaujon, the same hospital where I've had my hernia operation. He wants to express his admiration for the Americans, and I am the undeserving personification.

My 82-year-old trainer is not here today.

I hang around, using the machines, feeling especially strong but lamenting the absence of Alain *le poète* and my weightlifting trainer.

Two casual friends who may have reached the end of their roads. I think of my own end of the road, thankful that it's not happening today.

I did not find the random friends I was looking for, but I did find a stray couple from Eugene, Oregon with a wrench.

An obscure melody seeps into my mind, a Roland Hanna song called "Synchronicity," sung by his son Michael, which I came across by chance on YouTube, and became one of the 26 viewers: "illusions haunting me or is it synchronicty?"

Day 35: 25 km. Trip to date: 935 km.

Day 36

Fernman

I have an upcoming dermatologist appointment, and her words have influenced today's choice of route. I must become a human fern and avoid the sun, especially when it gets hot, and today is another of those days with yet another UV alert. On such a day, Boulogne is the go-to place, but what can I do there that's new?

Two activities come to mind: take binoculars to both lakes at opposite ends of the forest and sit there long enough to spot some new wading birds, or walk the bike on narrower dirt paths I have never explored.

I stop at the convenience store in Neuilly and pick up two sandwiches rated A on the Nutriscore to add to my mixed nuts and orange. Afterwards, I cross the only intersection that places me under the sun.

Once in Boulogne, I go to the large twin ponds on the east end of the forest. I wait patiently, but nothing happens. Wading birds seem not to like this pretty lake. Perhaps the rowboats have dissuaded them.

I cycle through dark corridors of the sprawling park to the pond at the opposite end and find a spot I've never before appropriated, under a tall redwood tree whose lower trunk is so smooth and shiny that if it had been a photograph, you'd complain that they'd enhanced it. I set up my picnic and the binoculars. The pond is quiet with no rowboats, and if I had long legs and could fly, I would certainly consider this spot for a long wade.

Just as I've settled, a young couple with bicycles approaches. It looks like they are disappointed when they see me, as if they had planned themselves to picnic under the sensorial redwood. We exchange greetings, and I note her Irish accent. He caresses the incredibly smooth lower trunk, as if he'd just done a perfect sanding job.

I take advantage of the opportunity to ask for a photo of the tree and me. She obliges, bubbling with a joyful Irish lilt, and snaps two photos, clicks in the digits of my email address, and promises to send the photos this evening from their hotel.

Until now, I've had a good percentage of successful photo ops, but this one looks sketchy. This is a romantic couple and sending a photo will not be their priority when arriving at their hotel room.

I eat slowly, giving a long chance for a cormorant, tern, or heron to swoop down to a poetic halt on the edge of the pond. Nothing happens of this nature, but the pond is still refreshing with its two swans and multitude of mallards.

Not giving up, I cycle off and explore some nearby paths on foot with the idea of later returning to the pond. I understand why Thoreau loved the woods, but I wonder how he would have reacted to the scene of a group of pole-toting Nordic hikers, now approaching me, most of them seniors.

I understand that using the poles activates upper body muscles that would not be used otherwise during a walk. What I see is that these poles successfully transition bipeds into quadrupeds.

Thoreau once mocked people lifting weights, linking the swinging of dumbbells to the taking of medicine (263). But the Nordic hikers would have been perceived as "in search of the springs of life," the essential for the hiker.

Once back at the lake, I check all the shores and spot no wading birds. I give up and decide to cycle back through the park along a shaded brook, the first return leg of my trip back to the hearthside. I've stored my binoculars deep in my backpack, having lost all hope of spotting the ultimate bird.

At a refreshing bend in the brook, with dapples of sunlight ever so faintly filtering through the canopy, I spot a heron: stretching his legs, elongating his neck, seemingly wondering if he should stick around. I perceive a clear blue tint in his feathers and wonder if this is a different type of heron. Too bad Armand is not around to give me a clue.

I should have kept the binoculars around my neck. I fear that in searching for them, I will move just enough to trigger a flap of his wide wings and a swooping up under the canopy to another wading spot, where his status as an introvert will not be threatened.

I freeze, preferring just to admire what I am seeing. How dumb of me to imagine that he would have set himself down near the rowboats or the mallards when he has this place all to himself. I get close to the intrusion zone, fearing that he will hear my breathing.

Then, perhaps without a thought (how do herons think?), he swoops up and away, and I can only catch a micro-glimpse of his flapping wings.

For the briefest moment, I chide myself for not traveling with a cell phone, if for nothing else to catch this magnificent bird in a photo. But none of my previous heron photos have been worthy of posting on whatever platform birders use to post their gems.

I have yesterday's photos from Armand. Today, it was probably best just to watch this delicate bird, who seemed to love the shade as much as I do, for as long as he allowed me to.

Day 36: 23 km. Trip to date: 958 km.

Day 37

A Steady-State Future for Farming?

I've waited for my ascent to the Butte Pinson because *La Ferme* (The Farm) is only open to the public on weekends.

From Montmagny, I ride upslope into a green hillside and keep climbing until I find an entrance into the dark forest. The path is rutted and full of protruding stones and roots, so I get off the bike and start pushing. Bike-hiking uses different muscles, so it's good exercise.

Here and there, a dapple of sunlight filters through into Fernville, but otherwise this hot Saturday has become refreshingly cool. At an intersection of dirt paths, I see an asymmetrical wooden sign on which *"La Ferme"* is artistically engraved next to an arrow, which I follow.

Managed by a non-profit called *Espoir* (Hope), this and other similar farms occupy degraded or abandoned lands, rehabilitating territories for ecological urban farming.

I am met at the entrance by *La Ferme* employee Alexandre, a tall young man who looks like perhaps he has roots in India. In secular France, one's roots are basically irrelevant, so I do not pursue my natural American curiosity.

Alexandre points to the wooden arch and fence around the entrance, explaining that all materials in the construction of the premises are recycled. Among the farm animals are some that have been abandoned or mistreated and are now given a second life. *La Ferme* is dedicated to permaculture and to combatting the system of food waste. Among the employees at *La Ferme* are some young people who opt to be here as an alternative to incarceration.

On weekdays, *La Ferme* opens its gates to schoolchildren on field trips and sponsors workshops for potential urban and peri-urban farmers. This looks like a last-gasp alternative to what Brian Czech calls "agricide" in his *Supply Shock: Economic Growth at the Crossroads and the Steady State Solution* (p. 17).

Alexandre invites me to take a tour, clicks some photos, then sends me out to explore on my own. I spot some free-roaming Rhode Island Red hens, triggering in me a moment of nostalgia for my micro-farming days on the high desert in California.

I am in another high place, on the top of the Butte Pinson (Pinson Hill), and at certain spots, I find an expansive view of the region to the north of Paris. I look for one of these panoramic spots for a picnic and find a colorful bench made of recycled wood, probably painted by schoolchildren.

From this bench, I also have a view of the goat corral. I recall my own experiment in peri-urban farming, where the chicken coop and each and every fence were constructed from discarded materials I had salvaged, but where my iconoclast goat was a picky eater. I feel at home, wondering whether educational farms like this will stimulate the creation of a whole new degrowth culture and then settle into a steady state.

I recall how I was the object of Department of Agriculture "employee humor" when I'd asked for permission to sell my fruit and produce. A DOA employee came to visit, got out of his station wagon, took one panoramic look at my small operation and broke out in a hearty laugh.

"You don't need any authorization!" he said, a euphemism for "How naïve you are!"

"This is too small. You can sell your produce to Korean grocers."

I learned from him that a normal-sized paper bag would contain the equivalent of a lug of produce and would be accepted as such by the small grocers.

I have no idea whether these educational farms can trigger a massive transfer from industrial farms to local agriculture, maybe a transcendent last laugh to the aggie employee who mocked productive gardening. Am I still naïve? The city of Montmagny could be an indicator, as it seems to blend city farming within an urban setting.

I walk the bike back down through the woods. At an opening, I see Alexandre and two companions eco-grazing the sheep.

Farther below, I roll by some of the home farming plots of Montmagny residents. The Center for the Advancement of the Steady State Economy (CASSE) briefing paper "Agriculture in the Steady State Economy" tells us that "Smaller, less mechanized farms produce more calories of food per calorie of energy expended to grow the crops."

By their looks, the Montmagny gardens are getting a lot of produce from their small plots, and the gardeners themselves are keeping in good shape. What's good for personal health is also good for the Earth.

La Ferme is promoting the localization of agriculture with resulting strong relationships between consumers and producers.

I remind myself that the bicycle has allowed me to visit *La Ferme* without having to use manufactured fuel. I also recall that urban farming experiments in cities like Detroit employ cargo bikes to transport produce to local farmers' markets.

Coincidentally, along an alternate route back home, I find another happy team of eco-grazing sheep.

I wonder (naively?) if a steady state economy, led by localized farming, can spring forth independently and then gradually, almost serenely, displace the GDP growth model. An estimated 2,000 to 3,000 communities in over 50 countries are involved in the Transition Towns Movement. The more informal peri-urban agriculture I've cycled through in Taverny, Montmagny, and Montmorency, as well as the *Jardins Ouvriers* in Paris, Clichy, and Saint-Ouen are part of an unattached collateral support network for the growing movement.

A Department of Agriculture advisor may scoff when he compares the scope of the Transition Movement to more than 30 million acres of land in the USA alone dedicated to growing corn for ethanol.

I am assaulted by a cruel caricature: yours truly cycling on a pretty road through cornfields to prove, jubilantly, that metabolic energy is the bright future in transportation, while the thousands of acres that envelop me are producing ethanol to put more cars on the road.

Day 37: 24 km. Trip to date: 982 km.

Day 38

Third Chair Encounters

I will explain why this day, the day I reach over 1,000 km, must not be the last. As a slow learner, I've belatedly realized that something is missing, something elusive and still undefined.

I cycle up to the Arc de Triomphe for a symbolic finish, but I should have known that this is not right. My enriching 1,000 km should not be ending on a cliché.

I used to cycle by the Arc de Triomphe several times a week during my bicycle commuting days. Today, I get to the Arc on a cloudy day with rain in the forecast. I do several laps on a concentric street around the Arc to get the feel for this new two-lane bicycle roadway.

I finally stop the anonymous theatrics to get a picture. An Argentine couple, tourists, graciously take pictures for me. On Facebook, the good people who have been reading my reports could consider this image in front of the Arc de Triomphe as a victory.

I see a bike traveler taking a selfie with the monument in the background. I ride over, brake, and offer to take his picture with his bike. He's tall, young, slim, and looking like he's in the middle of some massive cross-European odyssey. Some adventurers like him do unsung videos, only seen by other crazy people who do long-distance bike touring.

He glows when I offer to take his picture. This is obviously his first visit to the Arc de Triomphe, so we make an odd couple. I look up at the old monster and see blocks of stone. But now, focusing on the monument through his eyes, it looks great again.

He expresses his joy at having arrived at "the most beautiful avenue in the world," and I refrain from telling him that Champs-Elysées is infested with pickpockets and that chain stores have muscled in to replace the smaller boutiques.

He introduces himself as Souchu, says he's from La Réunion, an overseas French department in the Indian Ocean, a mountainous island with great hiking trails that I've wanted to visit, especially to hike there with Martha.

I finish taking pictures of him at various angles, and he offers to take mine. The Argentine couple already clicked on the send button, and their pictures looked perfect, but why not!

Then comes my moment of stupidity. He answers two or three questions about La Réunion, we knock fists, and I am off.

I should be thrilled that I am eating up kilometers and passing the thousand mark, but I have missed a great chance for an interview: a fellow bike traveler who is probably in the midst of a voyage much more ambitious than my own. Perhaps he's one more inhabitant in an invisible steady-state network, an organic revolution of metabolic energy.

I should have interviewed him on the spot. Later, I can surely ask him questions via e-mail, but once again I have missed a moment that cannot be recovered, like the moment I missed by failing to attend the funeral of Madmoiselle Odette Simon in Bougival.

When traveling, these brief encounters are often followed by regret. We cannot get to know all our brothers and sisters on this earth, and it's not practical, especially for an introvert like me, to engage in accumulating friendships. What's more, brief encounters play a vital role in a loose web of human solidarity: Thoreau's Third Chair. Such meetings are far more possible when one travels by bike than from a car.

There is usually a sense of loss when these human contacts in bike touring end up with no lasting connection, but Third Chair encounters have a meaningful function. And sometimes, lost-and-found situations emerge organically, (fast forward): like on the night of the summer solstice, when Martha and I bumped into Anabel and Nordine, the long-distance biking couple I met on the Le Vesinet trip (Day Fourteen).

We ended up spending an amazing solstice with them, listening to a guitarist who sounded like Leonard Cohen while doing incredible jazz riffs, at a funky café called "The Essential" that could have been designed by the unlikely team of Henri Matisse and Edward Hopper.

For the most part, however, I will never again see the couple from Oregon, the *sente* jogger outside of Montmorency, Armand the bird-watcher, Souchu the bike traveler, Alexandre, rehabilitator of abused animals, or Nicolas and Aurélia, the artists.

Now it is time to do some steady-state scoring, to summarize the final accounts on my journey, as Thoreau did with his stay at Walden.

I arrive home having completed 1,002 km. Yes, I have proven that travel, as it was in Thoreau's *Walking*, can be re-localized, thereby drastically cutting CO_2 emissions. I've proven that human energy can replace manufactured energy for touring and trips. I've shown that age can be tinkered with through incremental exercise, perhaps increasing healthy life expectancy. I've made a good argument that the health of the human being and the health of the earth have a common path within a steady state way of life, liberated from GDP, and I've encountered fellow members of my species who are already living this serene way of life.

I've made my point.

However, this point needs sharpening.

Something's been left unfinished and I need to find out what it is.

Day 38: 20 km. Trip to date: 1,002.

Day 39

Something Other Than Happiness along the Marne River

My wife and I had not seen our friends Claire and Elie during the pandemic. Normally, we would invite each other to dinner, attend Attac demonstrations ("Change Our Way of Life, Not the Climate"), hike together as far as the Alps, and do moderately-challenging bicycle trips.

For cycling, Claire disliked the hills and during the first "Adagio" week of these 1,000 km, I'd discovered a beautiful flat route that she would love, so I'd phoned them to set a day for us to go bicycling.

Elie answered, which was strange since Claire always answered the phone. His voice was grim.

"That is sweet of you," he said, "but Claire is fighting for her life, and her death is inescapable."

Her cancer had been in remission for many years and just a month earlier, she was still riding a bike. Elie explained that this was a "lightning" cancer attack.

Within two days, she was dead. I took a day off from cycling to attend the non-sectarian funeral at Pere Lachaise Cemetery, around the corner from their apartment. The eulogies and the music were produced by friends and family. It was a remarkable ceremony.

Now a month later, I receive a phone call from Elie. He invites me on a bike ride over the route that he and Claire loved the most, along the Marne River, east of Paris.

This is the missing ride I had been waiting for.

I recall Thoreau's quote: "I had three chairs in my house, one for solitude, two for friendship, three for society." I had been focusing on the first and third chairs while ignoring the second one.

In the final years of his life, suffering from what turned out to be an untreatable illness, Thoreau found hope and solace through travel with friends.

I have often thought that a steady state economy, which intends to stabilize per capita consumption, can only do so when the pleasure of accumulation is replaced by the wonder of friendship, which has no money exchange attached to it. In his famous speech on Gross National Product, Robert Kennedy concluded that GDP "measures everything, in short, except that which makes our life worthwhile."

The bike trip with Elie will contain memories and melancholy, human energy and camaraderie, none of which will add to the GDP.

It will also require effort. His apartment, our starting point, is exactly 10 km from ours, so aside from the approximately 40 km round trip along the Marne River, there will be 20 tacked on. Back in 2019, I'd done a similar trip with Elie and Claire. This would be a way for me to share the sense of loss, the melancholy, but also the stage of moving on, the acceptance stage that eventually follows or co-exists with grief.

Elie and I have often been on a third chair, sharing our affinity for societal subjects. This ride on chair two helps us to find some balance while we flow together with the river. Claire was the one who would bring our conversation subjects to a more personal level, and she's not with us, neither today nor forever.

Along the Marne, Elie and I are involved with solving the problems of the moment rather than major life-and-death issues, and this seems to be therapeutic. Certain parts of the river, especially with the wooded islands, are stunningly beautiful. I have been here before with Martha and I miss her dearly, so I can hardly imagine how Elie can get through this trip without Claire.

But in the end, finding the right place for lunch and discovering local curiosities replace some of the melancholy. In his role as guide, Elie takes me to an industrial water plant which is emblematic of a city that de-privatized water service, the first city along this part of the river to go back to the old system of municipally operated water.

He takes my picture in front of a water wheel sculpture that looks like a bike wheel, and I can feel that it is good for him to assume the role of guide and good for me to let him show the way.

In the end, back in Paris, we part ways at the corner of Cours deVincennes and Pyrénées (where our son went to Maurice Ravel High School). The rain clouds are thickening, and I feel a stray drop here and there. Thunderstorms are predicted, and I am forced to pedal as if I were in a race for survival, up Boulevard Voltaire, Boulevard Magenta, past Montmartre, and down Avenue de Clichy, where the rain gradually increases in force.

This is a half hour where I employ the "unsustainable growth" UG method, prolonging the high intensity into what is temporary overreach for my body. As I ride into Clichy, I am close enough to the apartment to slow down, knowing that I have beat the lightning, and now getting a little wet is strangely rewarding.

My encounter with the lightning, in some form or other, is inevitable.

Day 39: 60 kilometers. Trip to date: 1,062 km.

The "Art of the Ride" journey overall:

Cities/towns visited (not just passed through): 24

French Departments visited: six, namely

Paris

Yvelines

Hauts-de-Seine

Seine-Saint-Denis

Val-de-Marne

Val-d'Oise

Postscript

Is the Thoreauvian Method of Bike Touring Viable in North American Cities?

Some readers may appreciate this book as a unique type of travel adventure structured around a Thoreauvian methodology. That's fine. However, I purposely chose non-tourist areas outside of Paris to make the point that you don't need to be living near great monuments to use a similar travel method from your own home.

In fact, it is profoundly environmental to "re-localize" travel, thus cutting down on air travel, gas guzzling, and other types of polluting activities associated with modern tourism.

In November 2022, I had the honor of giving a reality bike tour (one of my 39 routes) to health-promotion specialist John Simmerman. John's "Active Towns" website advocates "a culture of activity for all ages and abilities." He was on a European tour, documenting successful urban designs as part of his advocacy for active mobility infrastructures in the US.

If Active Towns and dozens of like-minded organizations and YouTube channels meet their goals, what I call "Thoreauvian mobility" will become a more feasible option in the US.

We can easily say that certain city prototypes lend themselves to the Thoreauvian method. Cities not overwhelmed by sprawl, such as

Portland, Oregon, and cities near easy exits with distinct geographic boundaries, like San Francisco, lend themselves to multiple-destination daily bike trips.

Some larger cities remain dense enough to allow for serial bike destinations, especially those with good bicycle infrastructure.

Sprawling cities are more daunting. But, if they have bike friendly transit such as Los Angeles, California, or Washington, DC, they can be fertile grounds for everyday bike tourism thanks to the possibility of taking the bike in public transportation (suburban rail, metro, or bus) to access a "trailhead."

The Geography Factor

Take any of the competent bicycle city rankings and one factor rises to the surface. Cycling cities in the north with cold winters do much better in the rankings than southern cities which are hot and humid for half the year.

For example, the top twenty bicycle cities ranked in various specialist websites have in common the dearth of hot-weather southern cities but share multiple qualifiers among cold-winter cities, such as Minneapolis, Chicago, and Madison. (Of course, other variables beyond weather must also be accounted for, especially the existence of a built infrastructure that enables utilitarian bicycling by eliminating the car-proximity fear factor.)

Once it's too hot to bicycle, there is little you can do about it, no more layers of clothing you can strip off. During heat waves, I've resorted to morning twilight departures. When it gets cold, however, you can find all kinds of add-on clothing for warmth and protection.

What remains is a challenging situation that Thoreau may have thrived on, given his rebellious nature: the classic peri-urban city plagued by big box shopping centers and mini-mall strip roads: ("strodes" according to urban engineer Charles Marohn, because they are neither streets, with attractive commerce, nor roads, with practical through-travel).

Thoreau's approach to mobility as an artform is especially necessary when navigating sprawling territory. The relative density of European suburbs (6,600 inhabitants per square mile) favors access to multiple destinations whereas the low average density of American suburbs (2,700 inhabitants per square mile) elongates the distances required for each destination (reason.org/commentary/examining-sprawl).

The art of the ride in American suburbs would involve a creative discovery of unlikely destinations within travel distance and an equally creative method for navigating the strodes or detouring around them. In some cases, it becomes an act of defiance, since the whole notion of sprawl is to expand distances beyond the realm of human energy, leaving us with only one choice: driving a car.

When longer distances become attainable for some, they exclude others. Sprawl is inherently undemocratic.

I suggest several methods for the neo-Thoreau followers who live in the most sprawling suburbs:(1) Create your own *coulee vert* (greenway) by designing a trip that hops from one park to another. Parks may only be feel-good Band-Aids but connecting them is step one to bringing back the woods, even if it means a zigzag bike tour.

(2) Discover where nature rebelliously breaks through the cracks in the cement, where she occupies space that was intended to exclude her, and document your findings the way Thoreau documented plant and animal life along his trails.

(3) Create your own trips where you are not supposed to go, a method that straddles Thoreau's *Walking* and his *Civil Disobedience.*

In planning for my bike trips in the US, I joined the Adventure Cycling Association, whose interactive online maps or paper versions are quite useful. Since my US cycling is usually in Southern California, I joined the Los Angeles County Bicycle Coalition, which provided detailed maps of the region. Most local cycling associations around the country make similar maps available. Such maps include bike facilities and amenities and will point out worthy destinations.

In the absence of bike lanes or trails, legally you have the right to become vehicular cyclists, and in the absence of extra space in the right lane of a road, you have the right to occupy the same space as a car, excluding freeways, but an American car driver who is forced to slow down behind you may not be aware of your legal right to be there.

According to StreetsBlog USA, a study commissioned by the Florida Department of Transportation "found that motorists and dangerous street design--not cyclist behavior--are the primary factors that put cyclists at risk" ("Cyclists don't break laws any more than drivers do," 2018).

The study did not show situations where complying with traffic laws actually makes a cyclist less safe. Traffic laws favoring cars over metabolic travel also make walking less convenient. I have no doubt that if Thoreau were walking today, he'd get a ticket for jaywalking.

The Thoreauvian method in American suburban regions can be viable, but only if bike riders are imaginative in their approach.

In planning for Thoreauvian cycling from American "trailheads," the best go-to sources are the hundreds of local bicycle associations, which can be easily found by simply typing in "bicycle" and city name in your search engine.

For example, Bike Pittsburgh (BikePGH) promotes its "dirty dozen challenge," conquering the 13 steepest hills around Pittsburgh. The Rails-to-Trails Conservancy provides information on the best local trails around the country, so that clicking on their "find trails" link will connect you with the "best trails" in each region (example: the 10 best trails in Washington, DC).

The non-profit Adventure Cycling provides perfectly-crafted all-purpose maps that include services like bike shops, mileages, elevation profiles, and even how-to directions (called bi-directional narratives).

These are but a few of the hundreds of national and local organizations that can help you plot your artful ride. One of Thoreau's many liberating ideas is to start your adventure from "the old hearthside." Thoreau advocates for us to engage in errant sauntering for "he who sits still in a house all the time may be the greatest vagrant of all" (260).

And when he writes, "go forth and reconquer this Holy Land from the hands of the Infidels" (260), what is holy is our natural and wild heritage, and the infidels are those who have structured our communities in a way that have immobilized us as we move from the couch to the bucket seat of a car.

The unholy religion is the sedentary lifestyle, and no matter where we are, we can begin to reclaim the territory around us. Even the shortest excursion can be approached "in the spirit of undying adventure" (261).

Acknowledgments

Direct inspiration for my project has come from Olivier Bleys' *L'art de la marche* (The Art of Walking), Brian Czech at Center for the Advancement of the Steady State Economy (CASSE), Al Norman's Sprawl Busters, John Simmerman's Active Towns podcasts and videos ("a culture of activity for all ages and abilities"), Paul Tranter's analysis of "effective time," Ryan Van Duzer's YouTube channel, and bicycle activists around the world.

I also owe thanks to other YouTube channels, podcasts, and websites, too many to mention here, that defend the rights of pedestrians, bicycle commuters, users of public transportation, and non-consumerist ways of life.

Inspiration also comes from non-profits and organizations that offer alternatives to the GDP growth model, such as GrowthBusters, the Real Green New Deal, the Transition Towns Network, and too many other groups to mention here.

Jake Mayer deserves special mention, for it was his Zen approach that put me on this road when he published my previous bicycle-related book, *Old Man on a Green Bike: Chronicles of a Self-Serving Environmentalist* (Wordbound Media, 2019).

My wife Martha has been a truly innovative partner in how to put together a non-consumerist way of life.

Bravo to Rosalie Bull for producing what I thought would be impossible: a clear and attractive map of my convoluted journey.

Thanks to Lydia Schubarth for her pre-editing and especially for catching an unobvious error that would have caused incredible aggravation, as well as Brian Czech, whose broad vision, clarity, and direct help have been vital. And my profound gratitude to editor, fellow bicycler, and expert in sustainability, Gary Gardner, for leaving no stone unturned in his careful steps into the furrows of the manuscript.

Bibliography

I. Readings to help embark on a twenty-first century Thoreauvian path

Rossi, William. Editor. *Walden, Civil Disobedience and Other Writings.* (A Norton Critical Edition, third edition, 2008).
Most of the quotes in *If Thoreau Had a Bicycle* come from this comprehensive and foundational book.

Smith, Corinne Hosfeld. *Henry David Thoreau for Kids: His Life and Ideas, with 21 Activities* (Chicago Review Press, 2016).
I got this book for my grandson but it's a good read for adults, as it makes Thoreau come alive in contemporary times.

Thoreau, Henry David. "Life Without Principle." *Atlantic Monthly,* October, 1863.
In this seminal piece, Thoreau argues that the value of a thing is not defined by how much it will fetch in the market. Long before the advent of GNP (or GDP), Thoreau condemned the exchange of money as an indicator of wellbeing. This essay can be retrieved online at no cost: https://www.thoreau-online.org/life-without-principle.html.

The Thoreau quote cited in this volume about how a wanderer and an industrialist are viewed differently in relationship to the woods (see final paragraph of the Introduction, page 10) comes from page two of the *Atlantic Monthly* article. Thoreau's writing is freely available online at https://www.thoreauonline.org/.

II. Selected bibliography of some modern visionaries

Club of Rome. *The Limits to Growth.* (Potomac Associates,1972).
MIT researchers' findings on the impossibilty of unending economic growth. The book concludes that humanity can live indefinitely on earth if we impose limits on ourselves and our production of material goods. This would help to achieve a state of global equilibrium with population and production in careful balance with the capacity of the earth's natural systems.

Czech, Brian. *Supply Shock: Economic Growth at the Crossroads and a Steady State Solution* (New Society Publishers, 2013).
This volume ably lays out the rationale for the steady state economy. Czech founded the Center for the Advancement of the Steady State Economy (CASSE) in 2003. He served as the first conservation biologist in the history of the USA. He has been designated an "eco-champion" by Public Employees for Environmental Responsibility, an "eco-hero" by Ecohearth, and one of the "top 100 inspirational leaders" by the Post-Growth Institute.

Daly, Herman. *Beyond Growth: the Economics of Sustainable Development* (Beacon Press, 1996), and *Steady State Economics* (2nd Edition, Island Press, 1991).
These volumes are representative of Daly's foundational work on the steady state economy. Daly was an emeritus professor at the University of Maryland. From 1988 to 1994 he was a senior economist with the World Bank. He served on the boards of directors of numerous environmental organizations and was a co-founder and associate editor of the journal *Ecological Economics*.

In 1996, he received Sweden's Honorary Right Livelihood Award for Environmental Science.

Gardner, Gary. *The Earth Cries Out: How Faith Communities Meet the Challenges of Sustainability* (Orbis Books, 2021).
Gardner portrays some of the best practices of faith communities responding to the climate and sustainability emergency and in the process stimulates thinking about faith-group involvement in creating a sustainable civilization.

Hopkins, Rob. *The Transition Handbook: From Oil Dependency to Local Resilience* (Chelsea Green Publishing, 2014).
This book offers hands-on approaches to creating alternatives to a collapse into dystopia. Even if you disagree on whether there is a peak in energy, we still live on a finite planet that suffers from ecological overshoot. This book enfranchises us to act now rather than wait for politicians.

Illich, Ivan. *Energy and Equity* (Harper & Rowe, 1974) and *Tools of Conviviality* (World Perspectives, 1973).
With great vision, iconoclast Ivan Illich anticipates the wrong paths of the consumer and energy-addicted society and shows us how to re-direct our way of life.

Jackson, Tim. *Prosperity Without Growth: Economics for a Finite Planet* (Routledge, 2009).
"A piercing challenge to conventional economics" and a milestone in the debate on sustainability. Jackson was awarded the Hillary Laureate in 2016, for exceptional international leadership.

Latouche, Serge. *Farewell to Growth* (Polity, 2010).
Latouche is one of the triggers of the French degrowth movement. Knowing that "degrowth" was a loaded term, he refashioned the perspective to "abundant frugality." Original title in French: *Le pari de la décroissance: penser et consommer autrement pour une révolution culturelle.*

Powers, William. *Dispatches from the Sweet Life* (New World Library, 2018), *New Slow City: Living Simply in the World's Fastest City* (New World Library, 2014) and *Twelve by Twelve: A One-Room Cabin Off the Grid and Beyond the American Dream* (New World Library: 2010).
These works contain engaging and illuminating storytelling in which the author, much like Thoreau, experiments with paths to a non-consumerist, ecological way of life, developing theory through practice.

Schumacher, E.F. *Small is Beautiful: Economics as if People Mattered* (Blond & Briggs, 1973, and later HarperCollins, 2010).
One of the first economists to counter the mainstream ethos that "bigger is better." This type of critique had been anticipated by Thoreau, of course, more than a century earlier.

Tranter, Paul and Tolley, Rodney. *Slow Cities: Conquering our Speed Addiction for Health and Sustainability* (Elsevier: 2020).
Our speed addiction is every bit as destructive as dependence on speed of the other sort. As with most destructive behaviors, the excuse is economic, but Tranter and Tolley point out that this too is illusory. Slow cities foster cafe economies: resilient, small-scale, healthy, with far lower health, land, infrastructure and transport costs. Plus there's the economic benefit of actually surviving.

Walker, Peter. *How Cycling Can Save the World* (TarcherPerigree, 2017).
Walker takes readers on a tour of cities like Copenhagen and Utrecht, where every day cycling has taken root, demonstrating cycling's proven effect on reducing smog and obesity, and improving quality of life and mental health. Interviews with public figures provide case studies on how it can be done and prove that you can make a big change with just a few cycling lanes and a paradigm shift.

9 781732 993365